Unvanquished

How Women of the South Survived the Civil War

In Their Own Words

by Pippa Pralen

"There was a land of cavaliers and cotton fields called the Old South. Here in this pretty world, gallantry took its last bow. Look for it only in books, for it is no more than a dream remembered, a civilization gone with the wind".

~ Gone with the Wind

TABLE OF CONTENTS

The Cold Winds of War

Many histories recount the drama of men and battlefields. Women's stories of war are not told. In this book we read their words, we see with their eyes. The excerpted letters and writings have been transcribed as written, with no attempt to change spelling to respect their authenticity.

In the American Civil War (1861-1865), women left at home faced incredible hardships of war, hunger and loneliness. Southern women bore a heavy burden.

The blockade of southern ports in 1861, ordered by

Abraham Lincoln, caused shortages of essential food staples. Starvation slowly descended upon the South, and women struggled to keep children alive.

Women were alone to face these struggles. Most men were far from home and the weakened Confederacy could not help. At times only a handful of loyal slaves was the southern woman's support.

Formerly submissive women were forced to manage farms and plantations. Southern belles were catapulted out of their worlds of privilege.

In the following diaries we enter briefly into their world: the grinding struggle for survival, the terror, the cataclysmic upheaval of war. Slaves tell their stories too, as their worlds are turned upside down.

These resourceful southern women outwit the plundering Yankees when they can. Their lives depended on it.

Sherman's March to the Sea

General Sherman's "scorched earth policy" was a dreadful experience. Atlanta burned, farms were laid to waste, smoking cotton fields surrounded destroyed mansions, railroad tracks were mangled. The following account from Eliza Andrews vividly describes the desperate conditions in Sparta, Georgia, (100 miles from Atlanta).

Eliza Frances Andrews
The War-Time Journal of a Georgia Girl

"We struck the 'Burnt Country'...I almost felt as if I should like to hang a Yankee myself.

There was hardly a fence left standing all the way from Sparta to Gordon...the invaders...had wantonly shot down (livestock) to starve out the people and prevent them from making their crops. On every plantation, we saw the charred remains... lone chimney-stacks, 'Sherman's Sentinels', told of homes laid in ashes.

...I saw numbers seated on the roadside greedily eating raw turnips, meat skins, parched corn - anything they could find, even picking up the loose grains that Sherman's horses had left."

Starvation loomed as a real possibility. Farms and plantations were stripped bare of livestock and produce by Yankee soldiers and marauders. Marauders were a destructive horde of deserters, stragglers, and runaway slaves.

While stricken with grief for fallen sons and husbands, women continued to till the land, find inner resources to feed children and keep generational homes intact.

Food Shortages

At the initial stages of the Civil War there were minor shortages of luxury items. Coffee, molasses, saffron and elaborate hats and hoops became limited.

Soon more serious shortages, such as flour and salt, made life a struggle. The price for salt surged so high that many farmers who raised hogs were unable to preserve them because they had no salt.

Starvation at Home

The farm wives wrote, "Famine is staring us in the face. There is nothing so heart rending to a Mother as to have her children crying round her for bread and she have none to give them." *Petition from Iredell to Governor Vance*, 1863

Local governments tried to provide food, but many people still went hungry.

Baltimore slave Martha Ann "Patty" Atavis
holding child in her care

Soon they would try drastic measures to
obtain food. The railroads could not
transport enough food to feed civilians. Tons
of bacon, rice, sugar and other perishable
foods spoiled in depots and warehouses.

Sherman's troops destroying railroad ties

Speculators

Many black marketers hoarded and resold items at enormous profits. The inflated prices contributed to a scarcity of goods. *The Richmond Enquirer* reported that one man bought and hoarded 700 barrels of flour. The government was ineffective in curtailing the hoarding. Runaway inflation exceeded 9,000 percent.

Here is a description of prices in Virginia. (The average female clerk earned only $65 per month).

"... flour sold for $1500 a barrel, bacon $20 a pound, butter $16 a pound... and a chicken could be bought for $50". ~Pryor, Sara Agnes

Destroyed Railroads Atlanta

Eliza Andrews
Washington, Georgia

Eliza's home was not directly in the path of Sherman's destruction, but suffered food shortages as did many Georgians. She describes the monotonous meals:

"We have nothing but ham, ham, ham, every day...It is dreadful to think what wretched fare we have to set before the charming people who are thrown upon our hospitality.

...one day we have pea soup, another, pea croquettes, then baked peas and ham, and so on, through the whole gamut, but alas! they are cornfield peas still, and often not enough of even them.

... if it were not for the nice home-made butter and milk, and father's fine old Catawba wine and brandy, there would be literally nothing to redeem the family larder from bankruptcy." Andrews, Eliza Frances, *The War-Time Journal of a Georgia Girl, 1864-1865*

Clothing

When fashion suffered due to naval blockades, women used popcorn as hat decorations. Looms were taken out of attics and homespun fabrics became the rage. Worn garments were trimmed with piping to disguise the holes and tears.

Laura Elizabeth Lee
North Carolina
Laura was a relative of General Robert E. Lee:

"Every Southern woman wanted to show her loyalty to the Southern cause by wearing everything home-made, and store goods were tabooed as something entirely unnecessary". *Forget-me-nots of the Civil War; A Romance, Containing Reminiscences and Original Letters of Two Confederate Soldiers*

Old shirts and mattresses were unraveled, dyed with walnut hulls and woven into clothing. Old curtains and table cloths were cut and made into dresses. "Mend and patch" was the new motto.

Fuel: As fuel became more and more scarce, residents relied on winter clothes for warmth. Clothes became worn and tattered.

Fences were ripped down and pieces of wooden buildings were used as fuel as the cold became unbearable. People all over the South donated their woolens to the soldiers. Soon families at home were cutting blankets out of carpets.

Hoarding

At the beginning, women assumed the blockades would cease. Gradually women realized this was not the case. Eventually stores ran out of goods. Women with the means to do so, hoarded goods.

Mary Greenhow Lee
1862, Winchester, Virginia
"The incessant struggle to get enough food to keep us from starving is one of the hardest trials."

Mary bought and stored 200 pounds of sugar, 100 herrings, 25 pounds of molasses, and coffee and other items.

When the armies retreated, discarded food items were often strewn on roadways. Residents moved quickly, gathering the abandoned food. Foraging for food in fields

and forests added to the larder. Young boys
sat near streams, fishing. People learned to
hunt for any available squirrels, rabbits, and
other wild game they could find to be added
to soups and stews..

However in some areas war reduced the wil game:

"No farmer dared venture within the lines—
no fish were in the streams, no game in the
woods around the town. The cannonading
had   driven   them   away."   *My
Day;Reminiscences of a Long Life: Pryor,
Sara Agnes Rice*

Ida Barker
South Carolina
Holidays lacked the luxuries of earlier days.
Ida's description of Christmas in Union,
South Carolina shows the resilience of the
south:

"At Christmas times during the Civil War, people
in Union did not have luxuries, at all. Union was
only a village, and the stores did not carry much
at best. Charleston was blockaded and even
Spartanburg which was not much larger than
Union at that time did not carry luxuries in her
stores, either in food or wearing apparel.

Those who had money could not buy, for [it?] was not to be had. Everybody had to use parched wheat, parched okra seed or parched raw sweet potato chips for coffee. Not even tea came in.

We used sassafras and other native herb teas both daily and at parties when the herb teas were in season. Some were good, but the substitute coffee was not. The darkies cut the potatoes up into small squares and parched them in the coffee parcher.

We had plenty of food during the war. The woods were dense & they were full of wild animal life, & the streams were full of fish. On Christmas the dinner tables were weighted Lincoln down with turkey & other wild fowls & many delicacies from the garden, field or stream". ...

American Life Histories: Manuscripts from the Federal Writers' Project, 1936 to 1940

Food Riots

Women begged in the streets and at the stores until begging did no good. Many had been driven to robbery to sustain life.

In cities from Alabama, to Virginia, gatherings often erupted into riots in which crowds of women, broke into stores, depots, and warehouses and carried off supplies.

In the town of Salisbury, North Carolina in March 1863, a group of 75 women armed with axes and hatchets descended upon the railroad depot and local stores, desperate for food. The women thought that the railroad agent and the store owners were hoarding flour, to sell later at a higher price. When faced with the angry mob, the storekeepers reluctantly gave flour, molasses, and salt to the women."

In December 1862, women from Greenville, Alabama became fed up with the salt famine. They marched on the local railroad station shouting, "Salt or Blood," and forced an agent to give up the contents of a large sack of salt.

Richmond, Virginia - Bread Riot
In April 1863, a "mob of women" desperate with hunger, marched up Main Street, entered the stores of the suspected speculators and emptied them of their contents.

Eventually Jefferson Davis appeared, spoke to the crowd, and calmed the women who left, reluctantly, with their stolen baked goods.

Richmond Bread Riot, May 1863

Here is a vivid description from Alice Pryor of her encounter with one of the Richmond protestors:

"She was a pale, emaciated girl, not more than eighteen... As she raised her hand to remove her sunbonnet and use it for a fan, her loose calico sleeve slipped up and revealed the mere skeleton of an arm...she hastily pulled down her sleeve with a short laugh.

'This is all that's left of me' she said. 'We are starving...we are going to the bakeries and

Sorghum was cheap, plentiful in the south, and often went by the name of "sorghum molasses".

Sorghum is thought to have been introduced to America from Africa, making its way over on slave ships.

Flour substitutes: Rice, rice flour, cornmeal, and rye flour.

Salt Substitutes:
Salt's most important use was as a preservative. In an age without refrigeration, virtually all pork and beef was preserved in salt brine. Other foods, such as butter, had to be salted as well.

One salt substitute was boiled sea water. Also, dirt from the smokehouse, added to water and boiled, from which salt was extracted. Wood ashes could substitute for salt as a seasoning.

Smoked Meat:

Southern cooks would slice meat very thinly and smoke it. They would pound fish flat and dry it in the sun, often without the addition of salt.

Tea

Tea was enjoyed by everyone during the Civil War period. When it became scarce, and inflation drove the price to $50/lb., the population tried various substitutes for this precious commodity.

The leaves of the blackberry bush, huckleberry leaves, and the leaves of the holly tree were dried in the shade and used to make a tea.

Confederate Raisins:

Peaches were used to make 'Confederate raisins.' The peaches were dried and then clipped with scissors. The "peach raisins" were often used to add flavor to puddings.

Spices and Flavoring
Spices, pepper, flavorings, vinegar and baking
soda were very scarce. Peach leaves were
substituted for vanilla; peach and cherry
leaves combined made almond flavoring and
rose taste could be derived from rose leaves.

Vinegar
Substitutes for vinegar called for molasses
and water mixed and left to stand for two
months. Another was blackberries, water and
molasses mixed and let stand in the sun for
two weeks. Ashes left after burning corncobs
or hickory logs became widely known as
substitutes for bicarbonate of soda for
leavening.

Many creative dishes were created using only
basic and available ingredients. Cabbage soup

was a staple dish, and oatmeal pie (see Civil
War Recipes section).

Milk: Dairy products, such as butter and cheese,
which had been imported from New England;
became scarce. Bacon grease was frequently
substituted for butter.

Other substitutes
Clothing:
Old clothes were dyed to make them look new.
Pokeberry juice was a common dye.

Handmade pants and dresses replaced
imports made of fine fabric. When the oil for
the city's streetlamps ran out, workers
replaced it with pitch and hard pine knots.

Light: In place of kerosene for lights, the oil
of ground peas was mixed with the oil of
compressed lard.

"Beef tallow was held in high esteem,
especially by those who, like my mother, were
so fortunate as to own a pair of candle
moulds, for a supply of candles was extremely
desirable.

The more general way of supplying light for the
household was to take several yards of wicking,

... wax it and soak it in turpentine, then take a bottle, wind the wicking around it, leaving a little at the top to be lighted, and as it burnt down, pull the wicking up.

Scores of women sewed by this sort of light, making clothing for the soldiers and for members of their household." Hedges, Pattie Wright, *Confederate women of Arkansas in the civil war, 1861-65)*

Shoes: Almost all the shoes worn in the South had been manufactured in the North. With the start of the war, shipments of shoes ceased and there would be few new shoes available for years.

Shoes wore out. The price of ladies' shoes rose to $50.

~~~~~~~~~~~~~~

Sarah Morgan, a young girl in Louisiana describes her search for shoes:

Sarah Morgan Dawson

Louisiana
A Confederate Girl's Diary
Born into a wealthy New Orleans family,
Sarah Morgan began her diary in 1862 at age
20.

"I have had such a search for shoes this week
that I am disgusted with shopping. I am
triumphant now, for after traversing the town
in every direction and finding nothing, I
finally discovered a pair of boots just made
for a little negro to go fishing with, and only
an inch and a half too long for me...Behold
my tender feet cased in crocodile skin,
patent-leather tipped, low-quarter boy's
shoes...

What a fall was there, my country, from my
pretty English glove-kid, to sabots made of
some animal closely connected with the
hippopotamus!"

General Sherman

William Tecumseh Sherman

In the winter of 1864, Union General William T. Sherman led some 60,000 soldiers on a 285 mile rampage from Atlanta to Savannah, Georgia.

The purpose was, as Sherman said, "*to make Georgia howl*". They needed to "make old and young, rich and poor, feel the hard hand of war."

Sherman's troops captured Atlanta on September 2, 1864. This was an important triumph, because Atlanta was a railroad hub and the industrial center of the Confederacy. It had munitions factories, foundries and warehouses that kept the Confederate army supplied with food, weapons and other goods.

Sherman and his 62,000 men, fanned out in all directions, looking for food and booty. These feared foragers came to be called "bummers," and it was they who did the most damage to the countryside in their search for food for the troops. Operating under varying degrees of supervision, their exploits formed

Sherman's lasting reputation.

Whether it was a plantation manor, a more modest white dwelling or a slave hut, any residence encountered by these "bummers" stood a chance of being utterly ransacked. Barns, gardens and farms were overrun.

Bummers

"Bummers" was a nickname applied to foragers of General Sherman's Union Army. Supply bases were far behind, and the army's wagons could not carry provisions sufficient for all.

Sherman's soldiers were authorized to live off the land, and to leave each family "a reasonable portion for their maintenance." In regions where the army moved unmolested, no destruction of property was permitted. However, many disregarded these prohibitions. Too often, foraging parties became bands of marauders answering to no authority.

Some say the term "bummer" is derived from the German word *Bummler,* meaning "idler" or "wastrel". The bummers struck terror in the hearts of Southern people.

General Sherman is remembered for his cruelty.

The full story, however, may not be this simple. Certainly, Sherman practiced destructive war,but he claimed he did not do it out of personal cruelty. Instead, he sought to end the war as quickly as possible, with the least loss of life on both sides. He claimed he wanted to curtail the battlefield slaughter.

It is said Sherman wanted to wage a war that with minimal deaths. His destruction was focused on property damage. During his six-week rampage, fewer than 3,000 casualties resulted, much less than the 51,000 killed, wounded and missing at Gettysburg in three days of fighting.

> I am tired and sick of
> war. Its glory is all
> moonshine. It is only
> those who have neither
> fired a shot
>   nor heard the shrieks
> and groans of the
> wounded
>   who cry aloud for blood,
> for vengeance, for
> desolation.
>   War is hell.

by General William Tecumseh Sherman

The following diarists recount the experience of being in the path of Sherman's march:

Dolly Lunt Berge
A Woman's Wartime Journal: An Account of the Passage over Georgia's Plantation of Sherman's Army on the March to the Sea, The Century Co, New York, 1918

Dolly's husband, Thomas Burge died in 1858 of tuberculosis, leaving Dolly to manage the Mansfield, Georgia plantation on her own. Dolly witnessed *Sherman's March to the Sea* from her front porch and wrote about it in her journal.

"Sherman himself and a greater portion of his army passed my house that day...

To my smoke-house, my dairy, pantry, kitchen, and cellar, like famished wolves they come, breaking locks and whatever is in their way.

The thousand pounds of meat in my smoke-house is gone in a twinkling, my flour, my meat, my lard, butter, eggs, pickles of various kinds - both in vinegar and brine - wine, jars, and jugs are all gone. My eighteen fat turkeys, my hens, chickens, and fowls, my young pigs, are shot down in my yard and hunted as if they were rebels themselves.

Such a day... may God spare me from ever seeing again!

... the heavens from every point were lit up with flames from burning buildings. Dinnerless and supper less as we were ... with the fear of being driven out homeless to the dreary woods."

Irby Morgan describes the desolate landscape left by Sherman's troops.

Irby Morgan
How It Was: Four Years Among the Rebels,
Nashville, Tennessee, Publishing house,
Methodist Episcopal Church South, *1892.*

"While passing up the road we saw signs of Gen.
Sherman's work; he did it well and thoroughly.

It had been raining a great deal, and on the
clay hills were many tents filled with women
and children, with mud and slush all around,
and heaps of ashes, and smokeless chimneys
standing as lone sentinels in the devastated
and waste places".

Outwitting the Yankees

The Union Army pillaged, looted, plundered, burned houses. Livestock was stolen and crops destroyed. They shot chickens. They stole silver, and family heirlooms. As Ezra Adams, a slave, said, "they destroyed most of what folks had". *Slave Narratives Vol. XIV. South Carolina, Federal Writers Project*

Laura, a relative of General Robert E. Lee, describes a clever southerner who managed to hold onto his fortune.

Laura Elizabeth Lee
Forget-me-nots of the Civil War; A Romance,
Containing Reminiscences and Original
Letters of Two Confederate Soldiers

"After Sherman's main army reached
Raleigh, 'the bummers', as they were called,
followed in a few days...they stopped and
raided the home of Mr. Urias Baucom, a
former slave owner and stock raiser.

Mr. Baucom had made a great deal of money,
and had managed to convert it into gold. It
was an open secret that he had buried his
treasure.

These "bummers" had been told the story by
some of the negro slaves that he had
formerly owned. Going to his home they
demanded his gold; he told them they could
not get it, that he had worked hard for it and
would not give it up."

The 'bummers' hung Mr. Baucom by his
thumbs from a tree. He still would not talk.

Finally, his wife gave the hiding place of a
minor part of his fortune, a few old socks
filled with silver and a little gold, which

seemed to satisfy the foragers.

Mr. Baucom had never told his wife of the location of most of his gold, knowing she might not keep his secret.

".. they cut the rope and Mr. Baucom was a free man, but not many dollars of his hard earned gold had they found...

He had (previously) dug up the county road in front of his house, and taking his canvas bags of gold had deposited them there in the night time, then filled the hole with stone and gravel as if the road had never been touched. Sherman and his whole army marched over more than fifty thousand dollars of buried treasure in gold on the county road to Raleigh".

~~~~~~~~~~~~~~~~

Slave Views of Approaching Yankees

Slaves looked forward to the arrival of the northern forces, awaiting their day of liberation. However, for many slaves it meant hunger and suffering as the Yankees took all the food and livestock from the plantation. Some slaves grew to fear the northern Union army.

Ida Atkins
Former slave, North Carolina
Federal Writers Project

Ida recounts her first encounter with the Yankees.

The Yankees tied up her master and begun to plunder the plantation. Resourceful Ida used a clever ruse to outwit the ransacking Yankees.

Yankees and Bees
"Den dey took de knives ...and all de candle sticks and platters off de side & dey went in de parlor and got de gold clock dat was Mary Jane's grand mammy's. Den dey got all de jewelry out of Miss Mary Jane's.

Dey took de rings off her fingers den dey took her gold bracelet; dey even took de ruby ear rings out of her ears and de gold comb out of her hair".

Ida noticed bee gum tree branches which the Yankees had gathered and laid on the ground. (A bee gum is a tree filled with a colony of honey bees. This type of tree often dies from the inside out, and the bees like to build hives within).

Ida had an idea to force the Yankees to depart quickly. She quietly overturned each "bee gum" log. Soon the angry bees swarmed, attacking everyone in sight. The Yankees fled from the stinging bees, galloping out of the property, abandoning their stolen meat and pilfered jewelry.

The mistress was very pleased and told Ida:

'Ida Lee, if you hadn't turned over dem bee gums thee Yankees would have toted off near 'bout everythin' fine we got. We want to give you somethin' you can keep so' you'll always remember dis day man' how you run de Yankees away'.

Den Mis' Mary Jane took a plain gold ring off her finger an' put it on mine and I been wearin' it ever since."

~~~~~~~~~~~~~~

In the following account another resourceful, clever slave pretends that she and her daughters have "the fever".

Mamie Riley
South Carolina
Federal Writers' Project: Slave Narrative Project, Vol. 14, South Carolina, Part 4, Raines- Young, 1936-1938

Mamie was a slave in South Carolina. Her Mother used the clever ruse of telling the Yankees the "fever" was in the house. The men, including

Mamie Riley's father, had hidden in the woods.

"When the Yankees come through Mr. Solomons' place I was right there. ...I see it all. My ma tell me to run; but I ain't think they'd hurt me. I see them come down the street—all of them on horses.

My mother and my older sister was there. My ma grab a quilt off the bed and cover herself all over with it—head and all. And set in a chair there by the fire.

And she yell out when she hear them coming: **'There's the fever in here!'**

Six of them come to the door; but they say they ain't going in— they'll catch the fever.

Then some more come along. They say they going in. They ain't going to take no fever. Fill two sack of potatoes. White man ask to search all trunk. They take two of me Ma's good dresses out. Say to wrap potatoes in. I start to crying then, and they say, 'Well, get us some sacks then.' I knowed where some sacks was. I get them the sacks.

They do them right. They bid them goodbye,

and asked them where the man was."

The Yankees paid for what they had taken:

"They give me eleven or twelve dollars. I was little and ain't know. My mother never give it to me. "

Hiding Valuables

Southerners had a few advantages which ensured their survival:

1. Yankees often overlooked the patches of sweet potatoes, thinking they were weeds.

2. Southerners knew their local terrain better than did the Yankees. They knew its hiding places, and hid livestock such as pigs, in swamps and forests, and gold and silver in wells.

Estelle Laughlin

"A cousin told me the story of how her family's silverware, jewelry and precious keepsakes were saved from the Union soldiers by their servant, Adam. Word was sent by a neighbor's young houseboy that the Union soldiers were foraging, and so they had a little time to hide things.

"All the keepsakes that they felt the Union soldiers might take were hastily dumped into a large, dark-colored bag. Uncle Adam suspended it down into the well by the long rope.

The Union soldiers arrived and took the chickens, and some other things, but when they went through the house, they couldn't seem to find anything of value.

When the soldiers stopped at the well to draw up a bucket of cold water, the hearts of the watching family were in their throats, but by good fortune they didn't notice the rope suspended into the well, or else thought it was merely something put down in the well to be kept cold, as was the custom, and so the family treasures were saved." ~ Estelle Laughlin

Dolly Sumner Lunt Burge
A Woman's Wartime Journal: An Account of the Passage over Georgia's Plantation of Sherman's Army on the March to the Sea

Dolly was born in Maine. As a young woman she moved to Georgia, where her married sister was already settled. While teaching school in Covington, Georgia she met Thomas Burge, a plantation-owner and gentleman of the Old South, and married him. When some years later Mr. Burge died, Dolly was left on the plantation with her little daughter Sarah ("Sadai") and her 100 slaves.

Dolly describes General Sherman's attack:

"We have heard the loud booming of cannon all day...Suddenly I saw the servants running to the palings, and I walked to the door, when I saw such a stampede as I never witnessed before.

The road was full of carriages, wagons, men on horseback, all riding at full speed. Judge

Floyd stopped, saying: 'Mrs. Burge, the
Yankees are coming. They have got my family,
and here is all I have upon earth. Hide your
mules and carriages and whatever valuables
you have.

Sadai [Mrs. Burge's nine-year-old daughter]
said: 'Oh, Mama, what shall we do?'

'Never mind, Sadai,' I said. 'They won't hurt
you, and you must help me hide my things.'

I went to the smoke-house, divided out the
meat to the servants, and bid them hide it.
Julia [a slave] took a jar of lard and buried it.

In the meantime Sadai was taking down and
picking up our clothes, which she was giving
to the servants to hide in their cabins; silk
dresses, challis, muslins, and merinos, linens,
and hosiery, all found their way into the
chests of the women and under their beds;
china and silver were buried underground,
and Sadai bid Mary [a slave] hide a bit of soap
under some bricks, that mama might have a
little left.

Then she came to me with a part of a loaf of
bread, asking if she had not better put it in

her pocket, that we might have something to eat that night.

Sent off two of my mules in the night. Mr. Ward and Frank [a slave] took them away and hid them. In the morning took a barrel of salt, which had cost me two hundred dollars, into one of the black women's gardens, put a paperover it, and then on the top of that leached ashes.

Fixed it on a board as a leach tub, daubing it with ashes [the old-fashioned way of making lye for soap]. Had some few pieces of meat taken from my smoke-house carried to the Old Place [a distant part of the plantation] and hidden under some fodder. Bid them hide the wagon and gear and then go on plowing... I fear that we shall be homeless."

Laura Elizabeth Lee
Forget-me-nots of the Civil War...
Laura describes the anxiety and uncertainty as they waited for the arrival of Sherman's army.

"The next great epoch in my life was 'Sherman's march through Georgia', continued into North Carolina.

We were told every day that he would be there in a day or two, the days became weeks, and he did not come; everything was waiting for his coming, for we knew it was inevitable, and then began the hiding of everything of any value, but the children and negroes were kept in ignorance as to the whereabouts of the hidden effects.

I am certain my mother and her neighbors would hide the things one night and take them up the next to find a safer place.

Many things like silver plate had been dropped in the well or buried beneath the floor of the horses' stalls. A trunk containing clothing, my mother's wedding dress, especially to be prized, was buried in a pine thicket, a mile or two away from town.

Even faithful Aunt Pallas was not told where the things were hidden, lest through fear or threats she turn traitor at the last minute and tell the Yankees the hiding place".

Annie L. Burton Alabama

Memories of Childhood Slavery Days

Annie Burton was a slave in Alabama. The following is her account of her master's unsuccessful attempt to hide provisions from the Yankees:

"One day my master heard that the Yankees were coming our way, and he immediately made preparations to get his goods and valuables out of their reach.

The big six-mule team was brought to the smoke-house door, and loaded with hams and provisions. After being loaded, the team was put in the care of two of the most trustworthy and valuable slaves that my master owned, and driven away.

It was master's intention to have these things taken to a swamp, and there concealed in a pit that had recently been made for the purpose.

But just before the team left the main road for the by-road that led to the swamp, the two

slaves were surprised by the Yankees, who at once took possession of the provisions, and started the team toward Clayton, where the Yankees had headquarters...my master left unceremoniously for the woods, and remained concealed there for five days".

Buried Treasure
A Pot of Gold

Many a Southerner family buried their jewels, silver, and gold coins in the ground. Confederate soldiers died in battle, never to return to unearth the buried family wealth.

Martha Richardson was a slave girl in Columbia, South Carolina.

Martha and her brothers were working in the fields. As they chopped, her older brother's shovel hit something hard. He dug more and saw it was the lid of a pot. This discovery would change the fate of Martha's family. Martha describes what happened:

> "It was no sooner out than we takes off de lid and we is sho' surprised at what we see*
>
> Big silver dollars lay all over de top.

We takes two of them and drops them together and they ring just lak we hear them ring on de counters. Then we grabble in de pot for more.

De silver went down about two inches deep. Twenty-dollar gold pieces run down for about four inches or so and de whole bottom was full of big bundles of twenty dollar greenbacks."

They quickly return to their family cabin to show the pot to their Mother, who begins to empty it. She first tells the children to watch the door and see that no one enters. She counts the coins and tells them the money amounts to $5,700. *NOTE: this amount would be worth $90,000 today.*

She asks them to swear to tell no one about their find

Martha's family continued to work and later became sharecroppers.

With the newly found wealth, Martha's Mother bought 2 lots of land and built a house for the family and a cottage she rented out. Martha was eternally grateful for this money which allowed her family to escape from debt and to find some relief from their hard toil.

The Plundering Yankees

Like any conquering army the Northern soldiers plundered the southern homes they passed by. These departing troops left the southern homes in desperate situations, near starvation.

Eliza Frances Andrews

Eliza was born to a prominent judge and planter in Washington, Georgia. Her family owned two hundred slaves. She was young, in her twenties when the Yankees arrived:

"...We had just finished eating and got into our wrappers when two rebel horsemen came galloping up the avenue with news that a large body of Yankee cavalry was advancing down the Greensborough road, plundering the country as they passed.

We hastily threw on our clothes and were busy concealing valuables for father, when the tramping of horses and shouting of the men reached our ears. Then they began to pass by our street gate, with two of their detestable old flags flaunting in the breeze.

I ran for Garnett's field-glass and watched

them through it. Nearly all of them had bags of plunder tied to their saddles, and many rode horses which were afterwards recognized as belonging to different planters in the county.

I saw one rascal with a ruffled pillowcase full of stolen goods, tied to his saddle, and some of them had women's drawers tied up at the bottom ends, filled with plunder and slung astride their horses.

There was a regiment of negroes with them, and they halted right in front of our gate. Think of it! Bringing armed negroes here to threaten and insult us!

We were so furious that we shook our fists and spit at them from behind the window where we were sitting. It may have been childish, but it relieved our feelings.

None of them came within the enclosure, but the officers pranced about before the gate until I felt as if I would like to take a shot at them myself, if I had had a gun, and known how to use it. They are camped for the night on the outskirts of the town, and everybody expects to be robbed before morning.

Father loaded his two guns, and after the servants had been dismissed, we hid the silver in the hollow by the chimney up in the big garret, and father says it shall not be brought out again till the country becomes more settled.

A furious storm came up just at sunset, and I hope it will confine the mongrel crew to their tents." Andrews, Eliza Frances *The War-Time Journal of a Georgia Girl, 1864-1865* New York: D. Appleton and Co., 1908

Anne Bell
Slave, South Carolina
"I was about ten years old when the Yankees come. They was full to the brim with mischief. They took the frocks out the presses and put them on and laugh and carry on powerful.

Before they went they took everything. They took the meat and provisions out the smoke-house, and the molasses, sugar, flour, and meal out the house. Killed the pigs and cows, burnt the gin-house and cotton, and took off the livestock, geese, chickens and turkeys." *Slave Narratives Vol. XIV. South Carolina, Part 1, Federal Writers Project*

Mary Ann Lipscomb
South Carolina

"When we heard that the Yankees were coming, we had the Negroes to hide all the horses but two, and to hide the cows and turn the hogs loose to ramble in the woods. When the Yankees rode up to the yard and got off their horses, we could easily tell they had been drinking.

We told them that our horses were in the stable and that the Negroes had fled in terror, which was true.

They ate up everything they could find and ransacked the closets and pantry.

They then caught the chickens, took the two horses in the stable and went away. The darkies came back with the cows and horses, and we got settled for the night. About nine o'clock, the Yankees came unexpectedly and took all the horses and cows. They killed the cows, and made our darkies help them to butcher them and barbecue them. The Yankees soon ate everything up and left with our horses." *Slave Narratives Vol. XIV. South Carolina, Part 1, Federal Writers Project* (Note: Mary Lipscomb was not a slave, but was interviewed in the Federal Writers Project).

Black Yankees
Some diaries describe "black Yankees", recently freed slaves who had joined the Yankees in their acts of plunder.

Susan R. Jervey, Charlotte St. J. Ravenel *Two diaries from Middle St. John's, Berkeley, South Carolina, 1865*

Susan and Charlotte describe the ransacking done by "black Yankees":

"The freed negroes from the neighboring plantations seem worse than the Yankees, are destroying and burning everything

around the village, the Yankees tore up all the ladies'
clothes and threw them out of the window;
ripped up the beds; took the feathers and
provisions mixed them up with the molasses -
such wanton destruction!"

Witness to War

The actual witnesses to battles provide us with a vivid sense of the anxieties, the terror of war.

Emma Balfour
Siege of Vicksburg, Mississippi

Emma was a member of the local aristocracy; her husband was a successful doctor and she was on close terms with the leading generals.

The siege of Vicksburg was intense. During the siege, Union gunboats lobbed over 22,000 shells into the town. Confederate commanders urged citizens to occupy caves dug into sides of hills. Both white citizens and their slaves labored with shovels. Over 500 caves were dug into the yellow clay hills of Vicksburg. Here is Emma's account:

"It was terrific! I was up in my room sewing and praying in my heart, oh so earnestly for our cause, when Nancy rushed up actually pale...

...About nine o'clock in the morning, the gunboats towed some mortars into range, and there was a rushing into caves... We went into a cave for the first time... Just as we got in several machines exploded... just over our heads, and at the same time two riders were killed in the valley below us by a twenty-four pound shell from the east side.

As all this rushed over me and the sense of suffocation from being underground, the certainty that there was no way of escape...then my faith and courage rose to meet the emergency, and I have felt prepared ever since and cheerful..."

The siege continued through the month of June, as supplies and food ran out. On July 4, 1863, the rebels surrendered, and the Union Army marched into Vicksburg. Emma's home was taken as military headquarters for the Union occupation force commanded by General McPherson.

Having to surrender was bad enough, but surrendering on Independence Day made things worse for the Vicksburg citizens, and they did not forget it for 82 years. Vicksburg did not celebrate the holiday again until July 4, 1945, at the end of World War II.

Rachel Young King
Diary Rachel Young
King Missouri
Saturday, May 16th, 1863
"I have just witnessed one of the most
heartrending scenes I have ever witnessed.

In the fall of 1861 our neighbor, William
McClure, went south with his stock, negro and
sons. His youngest son, Alvin, came back to
his mother.

He was soon made prisoner. After working as
prisoner on the fort at Springfield, he started to

try to go to his father in Texas... News came back that he had been caught and killed as a spy which was proven by his having plots of the forts in and around Springfield. His mother knew this to be false and did not believe he had been taken but this spring she heard more particularly that he had been killed and not buried, that his body was rotting in the sun some 35 miles from Springfield.

She took a wagon, charcoal and coffin and went to the place and sure enough there laid the decayed remains of her dear Alvin, her baby boy, the youngest and darling of the family. The flesh was all off his face and ribs. She knew the remnants of his clothes, the buttons, cloth and binding and his boots and says she knew his hands which were whole.

She rolled him on a blanket and brought him home. She kept his remains some four days before burying them. We all visited the distressed mother and sisters. Oh what sorrow they feel God only knows. He was 19 years, handsome and quite intelligent".

Myrta Lockett Avary
*A Virginia Girl in the Civil War, 1861-1865:
Being a Record of the Actual Experiences of
the Wife of a Confederate Officer*

"One lovely morning mother sat at an upper window shelling peas for dinner. The window commanded a view of the Petersburg heights and beyond. Presently she stopped shelling peas, and gazed intently out of the window.

The hills looked blue.

The hills swarmed with soldiers in Federal uniforms! We heard the roar of cannon, the rattle of musketry. The heavens were filled with fire and smoke."

...mother was shelling peas again - whiz! whack! a shell sung through the air, striking in Bolling Square. Whiz! whack! came another, and struck Mrs. Dunlop's house two doors from us. (Neighbors) ran in, pale with terror, and clamored to go down into our cellar.

We were like frightened sheep. I half laugh, half cry now with vexation to think how calmly and stubbornly mother sat shelling peas in that window...

Finally, ... we all went down into the cellar. There we huddled together for the rest of the day.....At last, when we had heard no guns for a
long time, we crept upstairs and lay down on our beds and tried to sleep.

The next morning the shelling began again. Shells flew all around us. One struck in the yard next to ours; another horrid, smoking thing dropped in our own yard. We decided that it was time to abandon the house."

Lucy Rebecca Buck
Front Royal, Virginia
Lucy was a typical southern belle, although her life would abruptly change in the war. The family estate "Bel Air" was in Front Royal, Virginia, a strategic military area of the Shenandoah Valley, and control of the town changed frequently throughout the war. It was a place of fierce battles. Lucy was a fervent supporter of the Confederacy.

The family's daily life would change forever in mid-1863. Lucy awoke one morning and went to her grandmother's room to dress. "No fire was made, no water was brought, no movement whatever downstairs". Stowe, Steven, *Keep the Days: Reading the Civil War Diaries of Southern Women*, 2018

The household slaves had left in the night, taking the horses with them. Soon the women were milking the cows, cleaning the house and dressing the children. Lucy and her sisters suddenly had to deal with household chores for the first time. Lucy cooks her first pot of pea soup and makes biscuits for the first time.

Visit of General Lee

On July 22, 1863, as the Army of Northern Virginia marched through Front Royal on its retreat from Gettysburg, Lucy's father, William Buck, invited General Robert E. Lee and his staff to Bel Air for refreshment.

Lucy Buck wrote in her diary "I shall never forget the grand old chief as he stood on the porch surrounded by his officers; a tall commanding figure clad in dusty travel-stained gray but with a courtly dignified bearing". Lucy and her sister played and sang Southern songs while he stood by the piano.

The Bel Air estate was situated on a beautiful property in the Virginia countryside. In many passages she expresses joy in the natural world around her: "To sit on the porch and enjoy the moonlight, to fish in nearby Happy Creek in the spring, to tend to the flowers in the garden, to ride horseback into the mountains."

At times she expresses frustration and ambivalence at woman's roles. On her twentieth birthday she writes: "And I'm a woman, repel the unwelcome thought, as I will..."Buck, Lucy *Shadows on My Heart: The Civil War Diary of Lucy Rebecca Buck of Virginia*, 1870

The status quo was changing and southern women were being pulled along the tides of change.

**Sarah Morgan
Dawson age 10**
(Louisiana, 1862 -1986)
Sarah Morgan Dawson provides valuable insight into the events in and around New Orleans before and during the Federal capture and occupation of the city, through the eyes of a schoolgirl.

"To be hungry is there an everyday occurrence.

For ten days, ...lived off just hominy enough to keep their bodies and souls from parting, without being able to procure another article; not even a potato... I am satisfied that two months more of danger, difficulties, perplexities, and starvation will lay her (Mother) in her grave.

Lilly has been obliged to put her children to bed to make them forget they were supper less, andwhen she followed their example, could not sleep herself, for very hunger."

Nancy Emerson
Staunton, VA 1864

"They told us that Crook's men were a great deal worse than they, & that was true, but they were bad enough & worse at some other places than with us.

At one of our neighbors, they took everything they had to eat, all the pillow cases & sheets but what were on the beds, & the towels & some of the ladies' stockings. One of them made up a bundle of ladies clothing to take, but his comrade shamed him out of it.

They then poured out their molasses, scattered their preserves & sugar & other things about the floor, & mixed them all together & destroyed things generally."

Mary Boykin Chesnut
Wife of Senator James Chesnut, Jr., South Carolina

May 2, 1865. – "Since we left Chester ... nothing but tall blackened chimneys, to show that any man has ever trod this road before. This is Sherman's track. It is hard not to curse him.

I wept incessantly at first. The roses of the gardens are already hiding the ruins. ....I shut
my eyes and made a vow that if we were a

crushed people, crushed by weight, I would never be a whimpering, pining slave."

Battle of Gettysburg
3-day battle, July 1, 1983 - July 3, 1863

Although the battle of Gettysburg took place in the North, there are more accounts of this battle than any other. There are many eyewitness accounts from women. They offer a rich, detailed description of Civil War warfare, and how ordinary citizens became embroiled in the war.

Gettysburg was a small town in Pennsylvania, with rolling hills of corn and wheat fields and only 2,400 inhabitants.

The residents initially seemed unaware that two huge armies (Union and Confederate), about 170,000 men, were converging on their sleepy little town. The fiercest battle of the war was about to ignite.

Tillie Pierce

At Gettysburg, or What a Girl Saw and Heard at the Battle

Tillie Pierce had lived all her life in the village of Gettysburg and was 16 years old at the time of the Battle. Her father was a butcher and the family lived above his shop in the heart of town.

Tillie witnessed the entire battle. She was in a class at the *Young Ladies Seminary school* when she heard the cry "the Rebels are coming!"

"Rushing to the door, and standing on the front portico we beheld a dark, dense mass, moving toward town. Our teacher, Mrs.

Eyster, at once said: 'Children, run home as quickly as you can.'

"It did not require repeating. .....I had scarcely reached the front door, when, on looking up the street, I saw some of the men on horseback. I

scrambled in, slammed shut the door, and hastening to the sitting room, peeped out between the shutters.

Tillie as young girl

What a horrible sight! There they were, human beings! Clad almost in rags, covered with dust, riding wildly, pell-mell down the hill toward our home! Shouting, yelling most unearthly, cursing, brandishing their revolvers, and firing right and left.

Soon ...ransacking began in earnest. They wanted horses, clothing, anything and almost everything they could conveniently carry away.

Nor were they particular about asking. Whatever suited them they took.

Sisters of Charity tend wounded soldiers
at Gettysburg

At the urging of her family, Tillie and some friends left the town and went to what they thought would be a safe farmhouse, Jacob Weikert's farmhouse.

Over 700 wounded and dying soldiers found

shelter in the farmhouse and barn during the battle. Tillie provided water and food to the soldiers and assisted the surgeons and nurses caring for the wounded.

On July 7, she went back to her home saying, "The whole landscape had been changed and I felt as though we were in a strange and blighted land."

Judith Brockenbrough **McGuire**
Alexandria & Richmond, Virginia
Diary of a Southern Refugee during the War, A Lady of Virginia

Judith and her family fled Alexandria when it was occupied. They remained refugees for four years, eventually settling in Richmond.

Judith's diary is one of the best civilian diaries, filled with rich details and shrewd observations.

"To-day our house seems so deserted, that I feel more sad than usual, for on this morning we took leave of our whole household. Mr. and myself are now the sole occupants of the house, which usually teems with life. I go from room

to room, looking at first one thing and then another, so full of sad associations.

The closed piano, the locked bookcase, the nicely-arranged tables, the formally-placed chairs, ottomans and sofas in the parlor! Oh for some one to put them out of order And then the dinner-table, which has always been so well sur- rounded, so social, so cheerful, looked so cheerless to-day...

I looked at the Capitol in the distance, I could scarcely believe my senses. That Capitol of which I had always been so proud ! Can it be possible that it is no longer our Capitol?...

We have no mail communication, and can hear nothing from General Johnston. We go on as usual, but are almost despairing. Dear

M., in her sadness, has put some Confederate money and postage stamps into a Confederate envelope, sealed it up, and endorsed it, 'In memory of our beloved Confederacy.'

I feel like doing the same, and treasuring up the buttons, and the stars, and the dear gray coats, faded and worn as they are, with the soiled and tattered banner, which has no dishonouring blot, the untarnished sword, and other arms, though defeated, still crowned with

glory. But not yet—I cannot feel that all is over yet."

"The morning papers give the Northern account of a battle in Gettysburg, Pennsylvania. It gives the victory to the Federals, though it admits a very heavy loss on their side;... We pause for the truth.

Accounts from Gettysburg very confused. Nothing seems to be known certainly; but Vicksburg has fallen ! So says rumour, and we are afraid not to believe. It is a terrible loss to us ; but God has been the Lord."...Many troops have passed here to-day, for what point we know not. Our anxiety is very great...

I dread to hear of others. Who of our nearest
kin may have ceased to live ? When I think of
probabilities and possibilities, I am almost
crazy. Some of our men are reported
wounded and in the enemy's hands. They
took manyprisoners. The cars are rushing up
and down with soldiers...What does it all
portend ?

July 12. The enemy is again before Charleston.
Lord, have mercy on the efforts of our people !
I am miserable about my poor little J. P., who
is on board the Chicora, in Charleston
harbor."

Soldier Accounts from the Battlefield

The following are descriptions of civil war battlefields, from a Union soldier and then a Confederate soldier.

Union Soldier July 2, 1863

"The field is covered with dead and wounded. Out here there is a stink unimaginable, it's definitely more than I thought when I signed up.

All I wanted was an adventure and a little

money at the age of 18, but now I'm figuring out that I've actually got to man up and get the job done if I want to survive. As I'm writing this there is very heavy firing to the right of me about 5 o'clock. By the sound of it it's coming right in our direction. I better get ready."

Confederate Soldier

July 3, 1863

"All my buddies signed up for the war, so I did

too. It seemed like the right thing to do,

protecting our right to use slaves on plantations. How else were our farmers supposed to farm?

Now I'm not so sure I can take much more of this. I've gained and lost many buddies, a few get a decent burial.

Today I almost joined those dead buddies as today was a horrific day for us.

I was under the command of General Pickett and he and General Lee had the great idea of sending about 15,000 troops toward Cemetery Hill...I hope they realize now that they are complete idiots because we just lost countless lives, probably close to 10,000 men.

...they just mowed us down... we were sitting ducks. It was a horrific scene, the noises, the smells.

I can't believe how lucky I am to be able to write this right now, today must be my luck day."

~~~~~~~

There were also 190 African Americans who lived in the Gettysburg area. Many of them escaped or hid during the invasion, but many were not so fortunate and were taken captive by the Confederates.

Georgeanna Woolsey
Letters of a Family During the War 1861-65
Georgeanna was motivated to serve as a nurse in Pennsylvania. She had little formal training, only 100 hours of training.

After the Gettysburg battle, she travelled with her Mother from Baltimore, Maryland to Gettysburg, a normal 4-hour trip which took 24 hours. She was eager to help and to get her hands dirty in a way she had never been allowed to before as a wealthy, privileged woman.

Georgeanna established a 'Sanitary Commission camp' near the railroad station in Gettysburg.

Although a Union sympathizer, she offered aid to Confederate rebels as well.

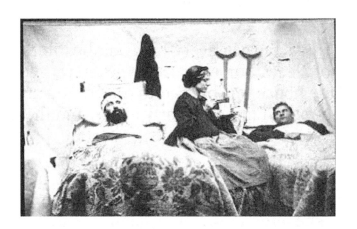

"I am glad we helped those rebels. They had just as much good hot soup, when our procession of cans and cups and soft bread and general refreshment went round from car to car, as they wanted; ..

We had lovely things for the men to eat —as many potatoes and turnips as they wanted, ...and custard pudding, and codfish hash, and jelly an inch high on their bread, and their bread buttered on *both* sides".

"Linnie Hutchinson
Standing up to the Yankees

Confederate women of Arkansas in the civil war, 1861-65

Years after the war Linnie's Uncle wrote of the bravery of this young girl.

"The Yanks burned everything combustible and not a cow, horse, hog, or chicken was left...the house was burned to the ground and the old man (Linnie's elderly uncle) and the young girl took abode in a Negro cabin.

Miss Linnie had practiced much with pistol and gun... when the Feds would come into her yard, she stood, pistol in hand, ready for anything.

One day a company of fifty entered the yard and began shooting every chicken in sight.

Standing upon the cabin porch and raising her gun, she declared that she would shoot the man that fired the next shot at her chickens.

They vacated the yard without further ado. She saved one old horse, old Mike, the buggy horse, but only after a fierce struggle in which several soldiers threw her round and round as she clung to the bridle until blood gushed from her wrists."

The suffering endured by civilians is almost unbearable to read. But this is War and cannot be completely sanitized.

Lutetia M. Howells
Clarksville, Arkansas

Sketch of Lutetia M. Howells by her daughter Sallie E. Jordan

"Five or six federal soldiers came and demanded money of mother, saying 'I know you have it, everyone knows your husband has plenty of money'. When she refused to give them money, they stripped the right foot and leg, and thrust it into a bed of red hot coals lying in a large open fireplace.

Her leg began to burn and still she refused to speak. The federals brought in her aunt and did the same to her.

Eventually their beautiful southern home was burned to the ground. The slaves tended to Mrs. Howell's wounds as best they could".

Unfortunately, her leg had to be amputated. Her daughter's grief at this events almost prevents her from the telling of this sad tale. When their family doctor visited her, he sunk to his knees at her bedside and wept. Mrs. Howell's survived another 2 years, perhaps weakened from the trauma of these events.

Confederate Cherokee veterans at Reunion, 1903, New Orleans

Cherokee Confederates

Some elite Cherokee Indians had African-American slaves. The Indians had a different attitude toward slaves. In many instances the slaves had a higher status than slaves of 'white' masters. They were treated more as equals.

The Cherokees and other "civilized" tribes (Creek, Choctaw, Chickasaw, Seminole) had previously been forcibly removed by the federal government. They distrusted the federals.

The Cherokees may have expected better treatment by the Confederate government. Many Cherokees allied with the Confederacy, joined the rebel army and fought fiercely for the Cause.

Virginia Cleaver
Reminiscences of Virginia Cleaver
Arkansas
Virginia describes the Cherokee Indian soldiers who fought with Maxey's brigade under Colonel Battle:

"The Indians had on their war paint.... When they were camped at the Two Bayous, the

(Cherokee) Indians frequently came to our house to eat, and enjoyed the lye hominy and sassafras tea we gave them. After eating a plate piled up with the hominy, they would pass the plates back, saying 'load up, load up'...And we did load up, in a hurry, as we were afraid of them".

Laura A. Wooten
Confederate women of Arkansas in the civil war, 1861-65
No More War in My Lifetime

"They (Yankees) spread general devastation. ...(they) took every horse, stripped the beds, stole the dishes from the pantry and then went to the smoke house and after taking the meat emptied three or four barrels of flour on the floor and mixed in a barrel of molasses. They ordered our negro cook to prepare dinner and tried to induce her to run away with them. She refused.

Then they plundered her house and took things of no earthly use to them. I hope that there will be no more war in my lifetime. The incidents that I have narrated are only a few of those that remain stamped on my memory.

Why the great army of the North should have made war upon women and children is hard to understand".

Treating the Sick

Another new role for southern women was as "doctor", since doctors were now scarce and ministering to needs of the military. Many substitutions were made for medicines and people had to forage the fields, searching for plant and herbal remedies.

For example, twigs of magnolia trees were used for toothbrushes and the LaBella or snapdragon was used for skin and stomach aches. Slippery elm tea was very useful for whooping cough.

Malaria

Malaria became a constant problem. Insects swarmed like a plague in swamps, marshes and bayous. Southern woman and children would smuggle much needed quinine and morphine from the north into the Confederacy in the bodies of dolls.

Quinine is normally made from the bark of the cinchona tree. It was used to treat fevers of all kinds, chills and the fever of malaria.

During the war the cost of quinine rose to $100 an ounce and was hard to acquire. The dried, inner bark of dogwood was used as a substitute. *Resources of the Southern Fields and Forests*, 1863, Porcher

Dysentery
A treatment for dysentery and similar ailments was made from blackberry roots, and ripe persimmons were used as well.

An extract of the barks of the wild cherry, and poplar were used for chills. For coughs and lung diseases, syrup made with the leaves and roots of the mullein plant (*verbascum thapsus*), globe flower (*trollius*), and wild cherry tree bark were thought to be infallible. Mountain laurel (*Kalmia latifolia*) was used to treat heart conditions and syphilis.

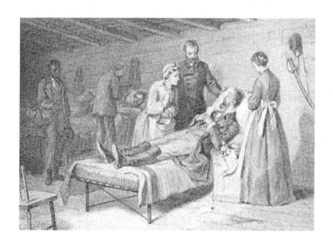

The Plantation Mistress

A common image of the Southern woman is the plantation mistress. An image of the lady of leisure hosting elaborate dinners and parties comes to mind, her main labor simply directing the duties of her house slaves.

Yet in reading their diaries we find these mistresses had diverse personalities and viewpoints. Many supported the institutions of the Confederate South, but some grew uncomfortable with the miseries of slavery.

The following account illustrates concerns a southern woman who heartily agreed with the established system.

Keziah Goodwyn Hopkins Brevard

A Plantation Mistress on the Eve of the Civil War: The Diary of Keziah Goodwyn Hopkins Brevard, 1860-1861

Keziah Brevard was a 57-year-old widowed plantation mistress, who lived some 10 miles east of Columbia, South Carolina. Brevard owned more than 200 slaves. She was terrified of liberating her slaves because she believed they were uncivilized. She recorded her thoughts and fears:

"Oh My God!!! This morning heard that Lincoln was elected. I had prayed that God would thwart his election ... the idea of being mixed up with free blacks is horrid!!

I have never been opposed to giving up slavery if we could send them out of our country ...if the North had let us alone — the Master & the servant were happy without advantages.

I never am cross to my servants without cause...but the die is cast. Let us all be willing to die rather than free our slaves in their present uncivilized state."

At other places in her diary, she recognized that the slaves are not happy in slavery. She erupts in anger "'when I find out their feelings to me — with all I have done for them   I am every now & then awakened by the fact that they hate me'."

Francis Hewitt Fearn
Diary of a Refugee

Francis Fearn was a woman who grew to

disagree with the southern slavery system. The diary begins in 1862 on the author's plantation in Bayou LaFourche, in southern Louisiana, just after the fall of New Orleans.

Francis attempted to foster a positive environment for her slaves. She established a hospital for them; her husband built them a church; and the family hosted balls and parties for them.

To escape the northern armies, the family moved to Alexandria, Louisiana, then Texas, and into Mexico before sailing to Havana, Cuba. From Cuba, they traveled to England and Paris, France, where they settled until the end of the war. They returned to live in New Orleans, Louisiana.

"Although I am a Virginian by birth .. I have never approved of slavery. It has been one of the greatest sorrows and trials of my life that my husband should own so many slaves...".

She describes a bond of trust between the Master and the slaves:

"Last year... he (her husband) called the negroes around him and told them that he was going off to be absent some time, and to their care and protection he entrusted their mistress and his child. ...

The night after he left.... I heard an unusual sound and got up to ascertain the cause of it.

As I opened my door I saw innumerable figures rise up in the moonlight, and a chorus of voices called out, 'Don't be afraid, ole missus, we are just here guarding you and the child for ole massa.'

I went back to bed feeling that we were safe in their keeping, but I lay awake many hours wondering what freedom would do for these child-like people. Would they be improved by it, or would they lapse back into a savage condition..."

Not every Southern woman was a wealthy plantation mistress of course. The following diary excerpts are from women of more humble means.

The Country Woman

Emily Jane Liles Harris

Emily's husband, David Golightly Harris, had been a small slaveholder in Spartanburg District, South Carolina. He owned ten slaves and 550 acres.

When her husband joined the state militia in late 1862, Emily continued writing a journal. She gave voice to the arduous lives of her countrywomen and the challenges posed by slaveholding as the institution of slavery neared its end.

Far from the idealized "plantation mistress,"

Harris faced numerous challenges, and not always with the best of humor. She wrote in 1863: "I shall never get used to being left as the head of affairs at home. The burden is very heavy   I am not an independent woman or ever shall be."

Despite her modesty and lack of self-confidence, Harris supervised her slaves, butchered hogs, planted her garden, cooked molasses, sheared sheep, and oversaw the planting and harvesting of hay, corn, cotton, and sugarcane.

She paid taxes, spun wool, and made sure that winter ice was preserved. She worried constantly about bad weather, the illnesses of her children, and the safety and comfort of her husband. At times isolated and at other times in need of privacy, Emily suffered from frequent bouts of depression, which worsened as the fortunes of the Confederacy waned and living conditions became harsher. "I expect no more rest this side [of] the grave," she wrote. "The wants of the family are never satisfied and their wants weigh heavily on me."

Relieved in 1865 by her husband's return from the

war, Emily Harris faced further challenges during Reconstruction. Much of the family wealth disappeared with the emancipation of their slaves, and some land was leased or sold to pay heavy taxes. David Harris died in 1875. Emily survived him and lived with her children until her death in Spartanburg in 1899.

Mary Gay
Life in Dixie during the War
Georgia
Mary's starving family desperately needed a horse, to acquire food. The federals had taken all the family livestock. Mary describes going to a canebrake swamp to look for a horse among the abandoned horses set loose and hidden from the Yankees.

"I had seen many horses, whose places

had been taken by others captured from farmers, abandoned and sent out to the canebrakes.

... Without any definite knowledge of the locality, but guided by an over-ruling providence, I went direct to the canebrake, and there soon made a selection of a horse, which, from the assortment at hand, could not have been improved upon.

By a dexterous throw of a lasso, constructed and managed by the young friends already mentioned, he was soon captured and on his way to Decatur to enter 'rebel' service."

Mary later used the horse to travel 40

miles round-trip to obtain food for her family and neighbors.

Mary describes their hunger and extreme measures to obtain food:

"We had spent the preceding day in picking out grains of corn from cracks and crevices in bureau drawers, and other improvised troughs for federal horses, as well as gathering up what was scattered upon the ground.

In this way by diligent and persevering work, about a half bushel was obtained from the now deserted camping ground of Garrard's cavalry, and this corn was thoroughly washed and dried, and ...ground into coarse meal."

Trying to Do a Man's Business

The following diary of Lizzie Scott Neblett reveals the unfamiliar roles she was forced to assume, restraining violent overseers, settling quarrels and supervising 11 slaves. It was a difficult time and she expresses her frustrations.

Diary of Lizzie Scott Neblett
Born in Mississippi, Lizzie grew up as a
southern belle in Texas.

When the Civil War ripped away the existing
social structure and took her husband away
from home, Lizzie was pressed to assume
many of his responsibilities, managing the
family property and its eleven slaves.

She also had to raise her 4 children. Lizzie felt
a growing sense of powerlessness and
inadequacy, and she frequently railed in
anger against her situation. Her children
were ill- behaved and as exasperating as the

slaves.

At the time of the August harvest she describes the slaves:

"the negroes are doing nothing... nearly all the negroes around here are at it, some of them are so high in anticipation of their glorious freedom by the Yankees I suppose they will resist a whipping".

Lizzie was forced to intercede between a violent overseer she had hired, Mr. Meyers, and the slaves. Early on the overseer had told Lizzie he could "conquer" her slaves but "may have to kill some one of them".

Lizzie was in a dilemma: she was dependent on the overseer, but not comfortable with the inhumanity of slave management.

Eventually, the overseer gave a slave an unprovoked, severe whipping. The young slave ran off.

He then threatened another slave, a man named Joe. Joe ran off through the woods, and soon appeared in front of Lizzie before Meyers could lay a hand on him.

Lizzie interceded. "I told him not to whip Joe, as long as he done his work well & that he must not shoot at him, that he might run away & we might never get him..."

The aspects of southern life that had been hidden to women; the dark side, the violence intrinsic to slavery, were now unavoidable, and women were forced to painfully confront them.

The overseer left at the end of the crop year.

Lizzie feared her slaves would seek revenge for the cruelties of Mr. Meyers.

Lizzie also took on the role of doctor. She applied her sewing abilities to stitch the wound of a slave who was gored in the hand by a wild pig. Lizzie disinfected the wound with sugar and turpentine, and then treated it with herbs; rhubarb, mustard plasters, peppermint leaves, cinnamon bark.

Yet Lizzie resented her forced entry into a man's world. She writes to her husband:

"I am so sick of trying to do a man's business

when I am nothing but a poor contemptible piece of multiplying human flesh, tied to the house by a crying loved one, looked upon as belonging to a race of inferior beings, as Swift says scarcely a degree above a monkey".

Lizzie's husband did return after the year. Work was now done by paid hired workers, not slaves. Their family wealth was a mere pittance now, the value of their estate had fallen by 60%. Lizzie was widowed at the age of 38, when her husband died.

Southern Invincibility

Many southerners had unrealistic views of the abilities of the Confederacy. The early views were that the war would be short and a grand adventure. That view would prove to be far from the truth.

Mary Chesnut
A Diary from Dixie

Mary Chesnut was a member of the elite part of southern society. Her father had been governor of South Carolina. She married a U.S. senator and Confederate officer. Unlike her husband, Mary secretly held anti-slavery views.

Like many of the planter elite, the Chesnuts

fell onto hard times after the war. They lost 1,000 slaves through emancipation.

Mary expresses her fierce belief in the Confederacy:

"We think every Southerner equal to three Yankees at least.

After his experience of the fighting qualities of Southerners in Mexico, he (President Davis) believes that we will do all that can be done by pluck and muscle, endurance, and dogged courage, dash, and red- hot patriotism. "

Ellen Renshaw House
*A Very Violent Rebel: The Civil War Diary of
Ellen Renshaw House*
Knoxville, Tennessee

Ellen despised the Yankee presence in
Knoxville and, on hearing that more Union
troops had arrived at Chattanooga, angrily
declared, "'I hope there won't be one left."
She was concerned that the Union army
"would like to exterminate the whole Rebel
population of the south".

In 1863, as southerners began to lose hope in
the war effort, Ellen refused to acknowledge
defeat and revealed her confidence in the
Confederacy when she exclaimed, "We are
not whipped, and never will be if the people
of the South are true to themselves."

General Lee's surrender was initially met
with disbelief. Ellen was utterly devastated
and abstained from writing in her diary for a
week before acknowledging that the
Confederacy was, in fact, not being
recognized and that the South would be
forced back into the United States.

The Confederate women's last hopes for the

survival of the Confederacy were dashed upon the capture of the fugitive president of the Confederate States of America, Jefferson Davis, by Union forces.

~~~~~~~~~~~~~~~~

Another optimistic Southern woman was Irby Morgan, who describes the fall of Fort Sumter as an exciting, glorious time.

Irby Morgan
How It Was; Four Years Among the Rebels

Mrs. Irby Morgan's memoir records her experiences in Tennessee. Her family fled across the South, stopping in North Carolina, Tennessee, and finally Augusta, Georgia, where they lived until the war ended.

She writes:

"The people of Nashville for weeks before the fall of Fort Sumter were greatly excited ...Fort Sumter fell; and no one can describe the excitement but one who witnessed it, and every one commenced planning and trying to do something to aid the South.

Drums were beating, fifes playing, the boys

coming in troops to enlist for the war, and anxious fathers and mothers could be met at every point.

All the old guns and muskets to be found were brought into requisition, and many consulted as to how to use them, ... but we went on the presumption, 'where there's a will there's a way,' to get us out of difficulty, and the result proved it".

Rose O'Neal Greenhow

Rose was the step-sister of Mary Greenhow Lee (mentioned earlier). Rose was a renowned Confederate spy. A socialite in Washington, D.C., she moved in important political circles and cultivated friendships with presidents, generals, senators, and high-ranking military officers. She used her connections to pass along key military information to the Confederacy during the war.

She was credited by Jefferson Davis, the Confederate president, with ensuring the South's victory at the First Battle of Bull Run in late July 1861.

Rose was fearless. Rose traveled from New York to Washington DC. when women were warned not to travel to, but she persisted:

"During my journey from New York the craven fear of the Yankees was manifested everywhere. At Philadelphia, most of the women got off.

A large force was distributed throughout Baltimore, and it was even difficult to thread one's way to the train on account of the military, who crowded the streets and the depot. Thence to Washington seemed as one vast camp, and on reaching the Capitol, the very carriage-way was blocked up by its panic stricken defenders, who started at the clank of their own muskets".

Pauline Cushman
Confederate Spy

A Brave Face

Many southern women tried to cheer visiting
Confederate soldiers on furlough. They did not
complain of the suffering on the home front.
They tried to raise the spirits of the soldiers,
showing only brave faces to them.

Ida Barker
Union, South Carolina
*Federal Writers Project, 11/10/37 ,
Interviewer: Caldwell Sims*
"During the war Union was as gay on the
surface as ever. When the soldiers came
home on furlough, wounded, maimed and

filthy, the women took them and cleaned them up, patched their ragged clothes and had parties and dances for them.

The women of Union could and did dance and sing and make merry with aching and bleeding hearts to keep up the spirits and courage of their men folks who came home so discouraged and blue in the face of defeat. Women in Union did everything. They never gave up and they never stopped making much with nothing

Women tried to alleviate the hunger of soldiers, who passed by their doors. When possible, organized food distribution was established for starving soldiers.

The Confederacy provided meager rations to its soldiers. Soldiers were forced to supplement their diet with hunting and foraging in the woods, and packages from home.

Colonel Frank Parker, of North Carolina, wrote to his wife in 1862 that "I shall await the arrival of your potatoes, sausage & c. with patience and shall welcome them with open mouths and good appetites."

A Gay Time Before the War

Plantation life before the war, was a gay time for many. They lacked nothing, tables were spread with delectable foods, and company was agreeable. The stately pillared mansion, at the end of long tree-lined road, was a symbol of plantation days. The manor house was only one of the buildings, there were many other outbuildings; barns, stables, warehouses.

Here are descriptions of the plantation days before the war.

Mary Norcott Bryan
A Grandmother's Recollection of Dixie (Documenting the American South, Univ. of North Carolina).

"The interchange of visits to other plantations was most agreeable, especially at Christmas time; we were always sure of a cordial welcome.

... what good dinners, large turkeys, old hams, home-made pickles, mince pies, syllabub and calf foot jelly, sweet potatoes

which we thought no meal complete without,
every delicacy the palate could crave, and
with it the kindest welcome to come again.

What a jolly time was hog killing, the delicious
hams put up by a receipt (recipe) handed
down from father to son and quite equal to
the Smithfield. The great pots of boiling lard
with a bay leaf thrown in for perfume, several
huge blocks of wood in the yard and fat
smiling mammies with red bandannas on
their heads singing sweet old negro melodies,
and chopping up sausage meat. The tom
thumb* is a thing of the past, so seldom eaten
now."

*Note: *tom thumb* is the name for a sausage
used in North Carolina. It is also called a *dan
doodle*. It is flavored with sage, and spiked
with red pepper.

Typical Plantation Dinner:
"For a dinner of 10 or 12, there would be a ham at the head, a large roast turkey at the foot, a quarter of boiled mutton, a round of beef a la mode and a boiled turkey stuffed with oysters.

In the middle of the table would be celery in tall cut-glass stands, on the sides cranberries in molds and various kinds of pickles. With these would be served either four or six dishes of vegetables and scalloped oysters."
Plantation Sketches, Margaret Devereaux

In less rarefied households, including those of slaves, corn and pork were staples. Many slaves were encouraged to grow their own gardens. Cornmeal, yams and rice were common.

Letitia Burwell
A Girl's Life in Virginia Before the War

"Time would fail me to dwell, as I should, upon the incomparable rice waffles, beat biscuit, and muffins, and marguerites, and flannel cakes, and French rolls, and velvet rolls, and lady's fingers constantly brought by relays of small servants, during breakfast, hot and hotter from the kitchen.

Then the tea-waiters handed at night, the beef tongue, the sliced ham, the grated cheese, the cold turkey, the dried venison, the loaf bread buttered hot, the batter cakes, the crackers, the quince marmalade."

Nancy Bostick de Saussure
South Carolina
Old Plantation Days; Being Recollections of
Southern Life Before the Civil War

"Father had hundreds of cattle, cows, sheep, and hogs. We milked sixty cows on the plantation... the negroes... came to the dairy to carry it to their homes in great tubs, and the little ones trotted along carrying their "piggins," which was the name for their small wooden buckets.

The milk which had turned to clabber, 'bonny crabber' as the Scotch call it, was considered a most delightful dish in our hot climate. It is so refreshing when cold that you often see me eating it now for tea.

Mother's vegetable gardens were ... so unusual in their beautiful arrangement that all strangers who came to the neighborhood were brought to see them.

.... I often used to hear mother say, "five hundred chickens, one hundred geese, one hundred turkeys, and one hundred ducks, were necessary to be kept on hand for table use."

Sara Pryor
My Day; Reminiscences of a Long Life
Virginia

"Dinner-parties demanded a large variety of dishes.

Three o'clock was a late hour for a dinner-party, the ordinary family dinner was at two. The large silver tureen, which is now enjoying a dignified old age on our sideboards, had then place at the foot of the table. After soup, boiled fish appeared at the head.

A list of dishes possible for a "genteel" dinner-party of twelve persons, soup, fish, eight dishes of meat, stewed celery, spinach, salsify, and cauliflower.

The meats were turkey, ham, partridges, mutton chops, sweetbreads, oyster pie, pheasants, and canvas-back ducks. Forms of ice-cream at the head, and at the foot a handsome pyramid of fruit. Side dishes, jellies, custards, blanc-mange, cakes, sweetmeats, and sugar-plums."

~~~~~~~~~~~~~~~~~

Supplying the Confederacy

Many of the supplies for the Confederacy; munitions, medicine, material for uniforms, came through the blockade from Europe. Blockade running became the lifeline of the Confederacy.

Mary J. White, age 15
Mary J. White Diary
Blockade Runner, North Carolina

Mary's father John White, a successful merchant in North Carolina, was commissioned to secure supplies for the Confederate army as a blockade runner.

He sailed out of Wilmington, North Carolina, with his family onboard the *Advance*. They planned an extended stay in England.

On these journeys, supplies from Europe underwent a sort of "transshipment" process, "whereby cargo was first sent from England and then reloaded in Bermuda or Nassau onto faster, smaller ships for the run through the blockade. Outbound ships often exported cotton, tobacco and other goods for trade and revenue

Wilmington, became one of the South's most important ports. Its proximity to the neutral ports of Nassau (570 miles) and Bermuda (674 miles), and the shallow waters in the Cape Fear River, made Wilmington an ideal port.

The Whites planned to leave from Wilmington and there to chance getting through the Federal blockaders and on to Bermuda and England.

To get through the blockade these ships, many of them built in British ship yards, were specially designed for speed. They had to cruise by undetected, usually at night.

For over a month they remained on board the *Advance*, making repeated attempts to run the blockade.

After nine failures, in which the *Advance* continually ran aground and faced hostile Union vessels offshore, White decided that the risks were too great and returned his family to North Carolina.

Soon afterwards, having made a total of eleven successful trips between Wilmington and Nassau, the *Advance* was captured a few miles from Wilmington

Mary writes:
"Aug. 15, 1864 –Smithville, NC. The *Cape Fear* came up just a minute ago and Dr. Boykin, Hugh and Tom have gone to see if there are any provisions on board for us. They just returned and say there are none. We are nearly out of bread and don't know where to get any.

This morning the pilot of one of the ships

lying in the river died of yellow fever... yellow fever is raging in Bermuda, so the *Advance* will not touch there but proceed to Halifax.

Aug. 16, 1864 –Smithville, NC. The boat came down today and brought abundant supplies of bread, bacon, pickles, corn meal, lobsters, tomatoes, watermelons, etc.... We went on the margin of the river and counted ten vessels lying in quarantine near here...

Aug. 23, 1864 –Last night at about 8:30 we started off to make the attempt. We went very well until we got to the inner bar and there, as usual, we got aground and while we were vainly attempting to get off, the moon rose and shone very brightly and then of course we were effectively prevented from trying any more.

After awhile, we got off and got back to Smithville, where we are lying now.

Sept 15, 1864 –*Warrenton, N.C.* On the 8th we made our 9th attempt and failed. We got to sea that night and the pilot had just given the ship over to the Capt, when it was discovered that we were about to be surrounded... She was anchored in sight of the Yankees all day, and everybody thought it would be so perfectly desperate that Father and Dr. Boykin took their families off.

The *Advance* got out that night, on the 10th. 35 shots were fired at her...

Father has decided not to take us with him as blockade running is so dangerous now....

Dec. 1864 –A few days after I last wrote in my diary, we were shocked to hear of the capture of the *Advance*. She was captured on Saturday, Sept. 11th, off Cape Hatteras".

Slavery

Different Perspectives

Viewpoints of slavery differ greatly. The slave diaries often tell stories of enormous suffering and horror. Their perspectives are quite different from the mistresses of vast plantations.

The lives of all southern women would never be the same. Plantation mistress, or field slave were both about to face cataclysmic change.

Some slaves feared the Yankees because many slave owners told exaggerated stories of the "devilish" Yankees. Not all slaves were fooled.

As the idea of emancipation slowly emerged, one saw more rebellion in slaves. It might be a slave's surliness or a slower pace of work, all new demonstrations of power.

Catherine Devereux Edmondston
North Carolina
Catherine, the wife of a North Carolina planter, accused her slaves of malingering in order to be assigned housework instead of fieldwork.

She believed in the concept of "proper station" in life, believing that women of African descent were expected to work from sunup to sundown in cotton fields. White women like herself were intended to care for dahlias, make blackberry wine, or decorate elaborate cakes for family celebrations. *Journal of a secesh lady: the diary of Catherine Ann Devereux Edmondston, 1860-1866*

.The lives of Southern black people changed immeasurably during the war years. They now faced extraordinary circumstances.

Many Southern slaves took advantage of the fog of war to escape towards freedom. They slipped across rivers and inlets to join Union forces. that were operating in Southern territory.

Vast columns of escaped slaves followed almost every major Union army at one point or another. These people, sometimes called "contrabands," frequently served as scouts and spies for the Union soldiers. (source: *Black Confederates, Truth and Legend*, S. Smith)

Faithful Slaves

Many slaves were loyal to their masters, having known no other life. They were also exposed to the southern propaganda of savage Yankees, heard from their masters. Some stayed on plantations during and after the war. These faithful slaves helped their mistresses survive, hiding family valuables, poaching food to stave off starvation, and outwitting the Yankees.

Slaves could never forget their status as property, naturally, no matter how well their owners treated them. Yet human beings who live and work together are bound to form relationships of some kind, and some masters and slaves genuinely cared for each other. (source: pbs.org)

Miss Linnie Hutchinson
Confederate women of Arkansas in the civil war, 1861-65

"There were twenty-five negroes on the Hutchinson plantation during the war and no white people except an old man and a weak young woman. The negroes were faithful. They helped on all occasions to hide things and never told the Yankees...

Old Aunt Sasa (slave) was a constant guard over Miss Linhie, frequently remaining up all night when danger was anticipated."

Some slaves were forcibly removed by the northern Union army. Dolly Burge describes her sadness at the forced departure of her slaves:

Dolly (Sumner Lunt) Burge
"...Alas! little did I think while trying to save my house from plunder and fire that they were forcing my boys [slaves] from home at the point of the bayonet.

One, Newton, jumped into bed in his cabin, and declared himself sick. Another crawled under the floor, - a lame boy he was, - but they pulled him out, placed him on a horse, and drove him off.

Mid, poor Mid! The last I saw of him, a man had him going around the garden, looking, as I thought, for my sheep, as he was my shepherd.

Jack came crying to me, the big tears coursing down his cheeks, saying they were making him go. I said: 'Stay in my room.' But a man followed in, cursing him and threatening to shoot him if he did not go; so poor Jack had to yield". *A Woman's Wartime Journal: An Account of the Passage over Georgia's Plantation of Sherman's Army on the March to the Sea,* 1918

~~~~~~~~~~~~~~

Nancy Saussure provides a touching account of a devoted slave who protected and cared for the Master's son who went to war:

Nancy Saussure:
"Another war incident in our family was that connected with a brother's son.

At the early age of fifteen, he ran away to go into the Southern army.

His mother could not make him return, so she called a young colored man, who was a devoted servant of the family, to her and said to him, 'John, go with your young master, and whatever happens to him, bring him back to me, wounded or dead, bring him back to me'.

He (the master) was finally wounded, and died in North Carolina in a hospital, John never leaving him.

After his death, John put him in a pine coffin roughly knocked together and started home with him. The devoted servant reached his mistress, having been two weeks on the way. He would tell his story ... to take his young master home, according to his promise to his mistress."

Myrta Lockett Avary

A Virginia Girl in the Civil War, 1861-1865: Being a Record of the Actual Experiences of the Wife of a Confederate Officer

This account relates the story of Hugh Bailey, wounded at the battle of Cedar Mountain, Virginia. His family thought he was dead, as they heard no news of him. A family slave nursed the wounded Hugh, probably saving his life

"An old negro, his body servant, had carried him off by stealth to a hut in the woods...to hide him from the Yankees.

He had no medicine, no doctor, no help, the master was ill for a long time from his wounds and with a slow fever, and through it all Uncle Reuben never left him except at night to forage for both. He was in a strange country; he could not leave his charge, alone and desperately ill".

Eventually, a group of Confederate skirmishers noticed the thin streak of smoke from the hut and investigated.

"The negro, the guardian in this instance was not anxious to have his charge moved. His whole concern was 'to git word to ole

Marster'".

The Confederates left some rations with them, traveled on and eventually sent a dispatch to the family of Mr. Baily".

A Florida party of Hugh Bailey's family was organized to come retrieve him. The party located him, "a skeleton of a man and the "gaunt, ragged old negro (who) followed". The party moved on toward Florida, but tragically Hugh Bailey died in Richmond.

Mary Boykin Chesnut
South Carolina

"The fidelity of the negroes is the principal topic. There seems to be not a single case of a negro who betrayed his master, and yet they showed a natural and exultant joy at being free.

After we left Winnsboro negroes were seen in the fields plowing and hoeing corn, just as in antebellum times. The fields in that respect looked quite cheerful."

Chesnut home, Mulberry

Chesnut's first meeting with Robert E. Lee

Mary describes in her own words how Robert E. Lee charmed her and her companions. At first Mary did not realize who he was:

"A man riding a beautiful horse joined us. He wore a hat with something of a military look to it, sat his horse gracefully, and was so distinguished at all points that I very much regretted not catching his name as Mrs. Stanard gave it to us. He, however, heard ours, and bowed as gracefully as he rode, and the few remarks he made to each of us showed he knew all about us.

...(he) said his tastes were 'of the simplest.' He only wanted "a Virginia farm, no end of cream and fresh butter and fried chicken - not one fried chicken, or two, but unlimited fried chicken."

... the man and horse and everything about him were so fine-looking; perfection, in fact; no fault to be found if you hunted for it. As he left us, I said eagerly, 'Who is he?' 'You did not know!

Why, it was Robert E. Lee, son of Light Horse Harry Lee, the first man in Virginia," raising her voice as she enumerated his glories'."

Theresa Millburn
Scribbing (diary)
Theresa Millburn was a young woman living on a plantation in Avoyelles Parish in central Louisiana. The following excerpt describes an altercation between her slave Oliver and a Yankee "negro".

Some slaves did not see the Yankees as "emancipators". Theresa tells of a slave who had fled and later returned to her, as he was tired of being with the Yankees.

March 18th, 1864: "The Yankees, in small forces, came ... I looked toward one of our Negro's chicken houses and saw them fighting - him and a Yankee Negro I screamed ... white soldiers ran into the yard. The Yankee Negro had wounded Oliver on the arm with a hoe. I never saw the like ...

Ma and I sat up all night ... and then the next morning: "we caught nearly all the chickens and turkeys last night and put them in baskets in the meal room and kegs in the dining room. I was never more annoyed by any little thing, than I was this morning about day light, by the crowing of the chickens in our dining room!

March 25th, 1864: A great many (Negroes) have gone, two from Uncle Morrison's, all from Mr. Keller's except six or seven, and all of Dr. Windes. None of ours have gone yet, but the one who left last Spring, slipped off and came home and says he's tired of following the Yankees. He is as polite as ever."

Slaves Who Fled

Many slaves, of course, longed for freedom. They had suffered under cruel owners and overseers and hoped for emancipation.

For many former slave owners, the prospect of freed men and women was confusing and frightening. Some reacted with rage, others with compassion and concern.

The following are accounts of slaves, describing the early days of the Emancipation:

Savilla Burrell
"Us looked for the Yankees on that place like us look now for the Savior and the host of angels at the second coming. They come one day in February. They took everything carryable off the plantation and burnt the big house, stables, barns, gin house and they left the slave houses." *Slave Narratives Vol. XIV. South Carolina, Part 1, Federal Writers Project*

Sara Brown
"I remembers the Yankees come there to my white folks' plantation one day and, child, there was a time on that place.

All them niggers was just a kicking up they heels and shouting. I was standing there on the piazza looking at them and I say, 'I don't see why they want to carry on like that for. I been free all the time.'

When they get through the Yankees tell them they was free as they Master was and give them so many bushels of corn and so much meat for they own. Some take they pile and go on off and some choose to stay on there with they Missus...". *Slave Narratives Vol. XIV. South Carolina, Part 1, Federal Writers Project*

~~~~~~~~~~~~~~~

Annie L. Burton

Clayton Alabama
Annie was one of the last remaining slaves on the Farrin plantation. Annie never knew her father who was a white man.

Her mother had run away 4 years earlier
after receiving a severe whipping.

Annie tells the story of her mother's love and
determination to retrieve her children from the
plantation mistress who was reluctant to release
them.

"All the slaves left the plantation upon the
news of their freedom, except those who were
feeble or sickly. With the help of these, the
crops were gathered...

Our mistress and her two daughters, Martha
and Mary, had to become their own servants,
and do all the work of the house, going into
the kitchen, cooking and washing, and feeling
very angry that all their house servants had
run away to the Yankees...The boys had to
leave school and take the runaway slaves'
places to finish the planting and pick the
cotton. I myself have worked in the cotton
field, picking great baskets full, too heavy for
me to carry. All was over! I now fully
understood the change in our circumstances.
Little Henry and I had no mere time to sit
basking ourselves in the sunshine of the
sunny south. The land was empty and the
servants all gone."

Note: Annie's Mother returned to retrieve her children. The mistress, however, would not release them.

The Mother hid and pulled the children through a hole in a fence.

Annie recounts their voyage:

"Then my mother took Henry in her arms, and my sister carried me on her back. We climbed fences and crossed fields, and after several hours came to a little hut which my mother had secured on a plantation. We had no more than reached the place, and made a little fire, when master's two sons rode up and demanded that the children be returned".

There was a tense discussion but Annie's mother prevailed. The family stayed together and was free.

"when my mother had got settled in her hut, with her little brood hovered around her, from which she had been so long absent, we had nothing to eat, and nothing to sleep on save some old pieces of horse-blankets and hay that the soldiers gave her.

The first day in the hut was a rainy day and as night drew near it grew more fierce, and we children had gathered some little fagots (wood) to make a fire by the time mother came home, with something for us to eat, such as she had gathered through the day. It was only corn meal and pease and ham-bones and skins which she had for our supper".

Her mother soon gained work as a cook and the children sold vegetables they grew in a garden. Their family was together. Annie never forgot her nights in the hut. Burton, Annie L. *Memories of Childhood's Slavery Days*, 1909.

~~~~~~~~~~~~~~~~~

Some slaves had mixed feelings about freedom. Life in the south was all they knew, except for a few old slaves with dim memories of being taken from a land far away across a great water.

Clara Brim,
former slave

Minnie Davis
Federal Writer's Project

"Mother was glad and sorry too that she was free. Marse John had been so good to all his slaves that none of them really wanted to leave him.

We stayed on awhile, then mother left and rented a room. She worked hard and bought a house as soon as she could; others did the same. There were very few slaves that had any money at all to begin on".

Fugitive African Americans fording the Rappahannock River.
Virginia, August 1862

Those slaves who escaped and were within the Union lines, faced several challenges. Women worked for the Union army as laundresses, seamstresses, nurses, hospital attendants, and even laborers on fortifications.

Many women and children were in "contraband camps," which were temporary settlements of former slaves located close to Union army camps. Some of these women raised crops for the government on farms confiscated from Confederate refugees. Women also tended their own gardens at the camps, raised chickens and hogs, and sold soldiers baked goods, dairy products, and produce.

In addition to the challenge of everyday subsistence, ex-slave women had to deal with such other problems as lack of warm clothing and good shelter, rampant illness (contraband camps had extremely high mortality rates due to disease), abuse from soldiers, and the transitory nature of life within a war zone.

After the Civil War, former slaves were promised a new life of freedom with civil rights. The newly freed women in the South had little or no money, limited or no education, and racism impacted every area of their lives. The transition from enslavement to freedom was a difficult and frightening one for most black women. To cope, many women helped eachother and drew on the resilience they had learned while enslaved.

The following 3 narratives describe the darker, painful experience of slavery.

Slaves Speak

The intrinsic cruelty of institution of slavery cannot be exaggerated. The suffering is staggering.

Slavery was an assault on the body and soul of human beings. Volumes of books could not do justice to the suffering. We have some recorded accounts of former slaves; many are narratives given to federal workers during the depression..

The following diary excerpts recall the viciousness of slavery and its sad history.

Mary
Reynolds

TEXAS
Mary Reynolds

Mary Reynolds was born in slavery to the Kilpatrick family, in Black River, Louisiana. She was interviewed in Dallas, Texas, where she lived.

"Slavery was the worst days was ever seed in the world.

They was things past tellin', but I got the scars on my old body to show to this day. I seed worse than what happened to me. I seed them put the men and women in the stock with they hands screwed down through holes in the board and they feets tied together and they naked behinds to the world. Solomon the [sic] overseer beat them with a big whip and massa look on.

The times I hated most was pickin' cotton when the frost was on the bolls. My hands git sore and crack open and bleed.

We'd have a li'l fire in the fields and iffen the ones with tender hands couldn't stand it no longer, we'd run and warm our hands a li'l bit. When I could steal a tater, I used to slip it in the ashes and when I'd run to the fire I'd take it out and eat it on the sly."

Mary relates the births of children of slaves fathered by the plantation owner:

"Once massa goes to Baton Rouge and brung back a yaller girl dressed in fine style. She was a seamster nigger. He builds her a house way from the quarters and she done fine sewin' for the whites.

Us niggers knowed the doctor took a black woman quick as he did a white and took any on his place he wanted, and he took them often. But mostly the chillun born on the place looked like niggers. Aunt Cheyney allus say four of hers were massas, but he didn't give them no mind.

But this yaller gal breeds so fast and gits a mess of white young'uns. She larnt them fine manners and combs out they hair."

Mary describes being unjustly blamed for a runaway slave:

"One day Turner goes off and don't come back. Old man Kidd say I knowed bout it, and he tied my wrists together and stripped me. He hanged me by the wrists from a limb on a tree and spraddled my legs around the trunk and tied my feet together. Then he beat me. He beat me worser than I ever been beat before and I faints dead away. When I come to I'm in bed. I didn't care so much iffen I died.

I didn't know bout the passin of time, but Miss Sara come to me. Some white folks done git word to her. Mr. Kidd tries to talk hisself out of it, but Miss Sara fotches me home when I'm well enough to move. She took me in a cart and my maw takes care of me. Massa looks me over good and says I'll git well, but I'm ruint for breedin' chillun." *Federal Writers' Project: Slave Narrative Project*, Vol. 16, Texas, 1936- 1938

Louisa Adams

NORTH CAROLINA
Louisa Adams

Louisa describes the constant hunger and their resourceful efforts to survive.

"Dad and mammie had their own gardens-and hogs. We were compelled to walk about at night to live.

We were so hongry we were bound to steal or parish. This trait seems to be handed down from slavery days. Sometimes I thinks dis might be so. Our food wuz bad. Marster worked us hard and gave us nuthin. We had to use what we made in the garden to eat.

My old daddy partly raised his chilluns on

game. He caught rabbits, coons, and possums. He would work all day and hunt at night. We had no holidays. They did not give us any fun as I know.

We left the plantation soon as de surrender. We lef' right off. We went to goin' towards Payetteville, North Carolina." *Federal Writers' Project: Slave Narrative Project*, Vol. 11, North Carolina, 1936-1938

Ex-Slave anonymous

TEXAS
Adeline Cunningham

Born in 1852, was a slave in Lavaca County,
near Hallettsville.

Adeline describes their crowded living,
sharing a cabin with another slave family.

"Dey was rough people and dey treat evfry body
rough. We lives in de houses all jine close

togedder (together) but you kin walk tween dem.

All de cabins has one room and mostly two fam'lies bunks togedder in de one room wid dirt floors. De slaves builds de cabins, de slaves got no money, dey got no land,.

No suh, we never goes to church.

Times we sneaks in de woods and prays de Lawd to make u free and times one of de slaves got happy and made a noise dat dey Leered (heard) at de big house and den de overseer come and whip us, cause we prayed de Lawd to set us free."

Adeline describes being fed as livestock would feed.

"Dey feeds us well sometimes, if dey warn't mad at us.

Dey has a big trough jest like de trough for de pigs and dey has a hit gourd and dey totes de gourd full of milk and dey 'breaks de bread' in de milk.takes a gourd and fills it and gives it to us chillun.

...we had oyster shells for spoons and de slaves comes in from de fields and dey hands is all dirty, and dey is hungry.we can't eat none of it. Dey dips de dirty hands right in de trough...

Adeline tells of the cruel fate of slaves who tried to run for freedom.

One of de slaves runs away. Dey catches anudder slave dat run way and dey hanged him up by de arm.

Yassuh, I see dat wid my own eyes; dey holds de slave up by one arm, dey puts a iron on his knee and a iron on his feet and drag ' im down but his feet caint reach de ground.

Ole man Foley ain't bad, but de overseers is mean." *Federal Writers' Project: Slave Narrative Project, Vol. 16, Texas, Part 1. 1936-1938*

Daphney Wright
SOUTH CAROLIA

"I been right here when the Yankees come

through. I been in my house a sitting before the fire, just like I is now. One of them come up and say, 'You know who I is?' I say, 'No.' He say, 'Well, I is come to set you free. You can stay with your old owners if you wants to, but they'll pay you wages.'

But they sure did plenty of mischief while they was here. Didn't burn all the houses. Pick out the big handsome house to burn. Burn down Mr. Bill Lawton' house. Mr. Asbury Lawton had a fine house. They burn that. (He Master Tom Lawton's brother.) Burn Mr. Maner's house.

Some had put a poor white woman in the house to keep the place; but it didn't make no difference. The soldiers say, This rich house don't belong to you. We going to burn this house!' They'd go through the house and take everything'. Take anything they could find. Take from the white, and take from the colored, too. Take everything out the house! They take from my house. Take something to eat. But I didn't have anything much in my house. Had a little pork and a week's supply of rations... The white folks would bury the silver. But they couldn't always find it again."
Federal Writers' Project: Slave Narrative Project, Vol. 14, South Carolina, Part 4,

Raines-Young

In the following account Rosa makes note of the loss of a family's wealth. Many southerners lost wealth accumulated by generations and never completely recovered:

Rosa Starke
South Carolina
"The Yankees come set all the cotton and the gin-house afire. Load up all the meat; take some of the sugar and shovel some over the yard; take all the wine, rum, and liquor; gut the house of all the silver and valuables, set it afire, and leave one thousand niggers cold and hungry, and our white folks in a misery they never has got over to the third generation of them.

Some of them is the poorest white folks in this State today. I weeps when I sees them so poor, but they is respectable yet, thank God."

Federal Writers' Project: Slave Narrative Project, Vol. 14, South Carolina, Part 4, Raines-Young

~~~~~~~~~~~~~~~

The Freedmen's Bureau
In 1865, Republican congressmen founded
the *Bureau of Refugees, Freedmen and
Abandoned Lands*, better known as *the
Freedmen's Bureau*, to avert mass starvation
and of freed slaves.

The Freedmen's Bureau, which had offices in
15 Southern states and the District of
Columbia, operated from 1865 to 1872 to help
manage the aftermath of the Civil War and the
freeing of slaves.

Children and the War

The Civil War had the effect of disrupting childhood. Children were politicized, and the anxiety produced by the hostilities that divided families and communities was profound for children. This, along with the violence and suffering they witnessed, left a permanent mark on them. Very few would emerge from the war unaffected by it.

The Civil War came right to their doors, and children learned what it meant to have an army descend on their farms and villages. It meant seeing soldiers in their stores, in their churches, and camped in their fields. It meant watching ambulances with wounded soldiers going through their streets.

Carrie Berry
Atlanta, GA 1864 to 1865

Ten-year-old Carrie Berry lived with her family in Atlanta, Georgia in 1864 while Union general Sherman tried to capture Atlanta. The diary that Berry kept daily shows the immediate effect of the war on her and her family.

"**Nov. 12**. We were fritened (frightened) almost to death last night. Some mean soldiers set several houses on fire in different parts of the town. I could not go to sleep for fear that they would set our house on fire.

Wed. Nov. 16. Oh what a night we had. They came burning the store house and about night it looked like the whole town was on fire.

We all set up all night. They behaved very badly. They all left the town about one o'clock this evening and we were glad when they left for no body know what we have suffered since they came in.

Thurs. Nov. 17. Everything was so quiet we were afraid that the yankees will come back and finish burning the houses but they did not. They have left. Some Confederates came in here today and the town is full of country people seeing what they can find. We have been picking up some things."

~~~~~~~~~~~~~~

Caring for the wounded, hiding horses, and having battles erupt in their midst affected children in another way; it displaced them from their schools. Schools near battlefields often became hospitals, and schools were forced to suspend classes for that reason. In Frederick, Maryland, the entire fall semester of 1862 was lost after the Battle of Antietam when schools were used for the care of the wounded.

Boys played mock battles, but some found ways to join the Union or Confederate armies even though they were underage. Although both armies stipulated that recruits had to be at least eighteen years old, sometimes older-looking fifteen- and sixteen-year-olds could get past the recruiting sergeants.

Life still included some joyous occasions such as Holidays. The following account of Christmas though, shows the lack of luxuries.

Dolly Sumner Lunt Berge
Mansfield, Georgia

"December 24, 1864
This has usually been a very busy day with me, preparing for Christmas not only for my own tables, but for gifts for my servants. Now how changed! No confectionery, cakes, or pies can I have.

We are all sad; no loud, jovial laugh from our boys is heard. Christmas Eve, which has ever been gaily celebrated here, which has witnessed the popping of fire-crackers [the Southern custom of celebrating Christmas with fireworks] and the hanging up of stockings, is an occasion now of sadness and gloom. I have nothing even to put in Sadai's stocking, which hangs so invitingly for Santa Claus. How disappointed she will be in the morning, though I have explained to her why he cannot come. Poor children! Why must the innocent suffer with the guilty.

December 25, 1864
Sadai jumped out of bed very early this morning to feel in her stocking. She could not believe but that there would be something in it.

Finding nothing, she crept back into bed, pulled the cover over her face, and I soon heard her sobbing. The little negroes all came in: "Christmas gift, mist'ess! Christmas gift, mist'ess!" I pulled the cover over my face and was soon mingling my tears with Sadai's."

~~~~~~~~~~~~

Slave Children

For slave children, war on the border areas brought extra dangers.

Benjamin Tucker Tanner served as a church minister in Frederick, Maryland. His son, Henry Ossawa Tanner, later wrote about his memories of the family's wartime experiences and how his father cleverly outwitted the soldiers.

Henry Ossawa Tanner

"From our attic window the rebel camp and soldiers could be seen."

Henry remembered that his father "took the precaution of nailing boards over the windows in the house to make it look abandoned and although soldiers passed by their house all day long, only one stopped to bang on the door".

A Kind Yankee

Not every Yankee was cruel. The following diary excerpt is a touching story of the kindness of a Yankee soldier to a southern family in Georgia.

Laura Elizabeth Lee
Forget-me-nots of the Civil War
Laura Elizabeth Lee lived in Clayton, Georgia near the Tennessee border. Elizabeth was a relative of General Robert E. Lee.

When Sherman's army marched through Clayton, Laura's mother approached General Sherman, who was on horseback and requested he provide a guard for her and her daughters, which he did. Laura had some good feelings about the Yankees, but still feared them.

In a attempt to acquire desperately needed food and goods, 10-year old Laura approached a Yankee encampment to sell some yellow plums she carried in a basket. There she met a Yankee soldier.

"'...he returned with two large pans, one filled with meat, bacon, and the other with loaf sugar.

'Oh, how lovely,' I said, but then remembering my mother, I became confused and said: 'Oh, I am afraid my mother will be angry if I take these things.'

My friend evidently seeing how disturbed I was, said: 'Well, Bettie, take them anyway, and if you won't accept them as a gift, bring me some lettuce or greens of some kind and your mother will surely not object to that'. I thanked him and asked him, 'Who shall I call for on my return?' 'Just ask for *Uncle Ned*'."

The family's hunger soon overtook their pride and resistance to trading with "the awful Yankees". Laura continued to sell vegetables and fruits to the Yankees, gaining needed income.

Uncle Ned also brought pretty dresses and shoes back from Baltimore, and other scarce items. His gifts and kindness offered her family some relief from their poverty. In later years Laura recalled her Yankee "Uncle Ned" with warmth and tenderness.

The Occupiers

During reconstruction and the transitional period, southern women had difficulties. With bitterness and hurt pride, women were forced to deal with the northern occupiers. Some women remained openly hostile to the Yankee occupiers. Other women feigned cooperation.

Yet, there were acts of kindness and compassion from Yankee officers toward southern women.

Mary Gay describes their first morning after the arrival of the northern army in Atlanta. Their home was vandalized by the vanguard of the army, and livestock stolen. The arriving Yankee officers expressed disgust at the work of the "vandals".

The first morning of the occupation, they awoke hungry, with no food available. A package soon arrived at their door from Union Army Major Campbell who she briefly met the day before, with a note:

"To Mrs. Stokes and daughter, Miss Gay, with compliments of (Major) Campbell. 'Please accept this small testimonial of regard and respectful sympathy.'

The contents of the tray; coffee, sugar and tea, sliced ham and a variety of canned relishes, butter, potatoes, and oat-meal and bread, were removed and   tray returned.

That tray, on its humane mission, having found its way into our house more than once opportunely reappeared. We enjoyed the repast thus furnished, although briny tears were mingled with it." *Life in Dixie During the War, Mary A.H. Gay*

Other southerners describe a more grim reality:

Diary Alice Williamson
1864, Tennessee
Schoolgirl Alice Williamson kept a diary of events in Gallatin, Tennessee. The main topic of the diary is the occupation by Union forces and the cruelty of General Eleazer Paine.

March 12th "Old Payne (Yankee General) dined at Mrs. Hales today: every one despises him but are afraid to show it.

Yesterday he went up the country a few miles to a Mr. Dalton's whose son came home from the Southern Army... riding up to the door he enquired of Mr. Dalton if his son was at home but before he answered his son came to the door.

Old Nick then told him to get his horse and go with him. He carried his son a half mile away and shot him six times... But this is nothing new this is the fifth man that has been shot in this way, besides numbers that have been carried off by scouts and never return.

May 20th Citizens are afraid to speak to each other when they meet. The yankees have said they should not talk together since the late fight in Tennessee."

Lizzie Alsop
Fredericksburg, Virginia

Elizabeth (Lizzie) Maxwell Alsop was born into a world of privilege. She began writing her Civil War diary in 1862 when she was sixteen years old. Her father was one of the richest members of the Fredericksburg community; a large part of his wealth consisted of slaves, 48 to be exact. Lizzie offers an adolescent viewpoint of the Civil War's turbulent times.

"We Confederates are, generally speaking, the most cheerful people imaginable, and treat the Yankees with silent contempt. They little know the hatred in our hearts towards them - the GREAT scorn we entertain for Yankees. I never hear or see a Federal riding down the street that I don't wish his neck may be broken before he crosses the bridge."

After the Union occupation of Fredericksburg in 1862, the Alsops decided to leave

Fredericksburg and go to their other house.
Lizzie wrote:

"Five weeks ago Father, Mother, Nannie
[Lizzie's sister], Mr. and Mrs. Allen fled from
Fredericksburg, thought to be in imminent
danger; and took refuge in this house
[Hilton, their plantation home in the
countryside of Spotsylvania County], and
here they have been ever since and are likely
to remain for some time.

During the shelling of Fredericksburg,
December 11th, 1862, very few citizens
remained in town, not more than a hundred
and fifty if so many. Uncle William and Mrs.
Foulke were at our house, but after the
Yankees crossed over they left.

The house... was very much injured, every
room rendered not inhabitable except two...

When any one asks Father how much they
injured him he says I can tell you much better
what they left, than what they destroyed.
However we fared better than some."

The Oath of Loyalty

The "*Oath of Loyalty*" was an oath that mandated the southerners renounce any association with the Confederacy. If they did not take the oath they often were denied access to food supplies.

The oath further demoralized the southern people.

Despite fear of starvation many women refused the oath and treated it with contempt. The oath further prevented access to supplies, restricting travel to "loyal" citizens. Therefore, residents trying to travel to areas with more resources were unable to leave.

Some women never took the oath because they felt it took their identities as southern "Secesh" women. They had lost much, sons, husbands, wealth, but they held fast to their culture.

For some women, however, this pride was a luxury they could not afford. The need to feed children forced them to appear cooperative with the Union. It was a further humiliation and a difficult burden to bear.

Direct boldness toward Yankees could invoke retaliation. Many southern women became the master of the cold stare, the condescending voice, the subtle insult.

Rachel Young King
Wife of William Sydney
Anderson *Diary Rachel Young
King Missouri*

Rachel's husband takes the Oath out of
necessity, but she refuses, and becomes a
prisoner in her own home.

July 1, 1862
"Well, what next? The whole community is in
a state of excitement. The Federal commander

has issued the order that all citizens are commanded to take an oath of allegiance to the Federal Government. Those who do not swear are not allowed to follow any business whatever and are prisoners at home.

This oath compels thousands to swear against their own conscience or have their families to perish. Mr. Anderson (Rachel's husband) this day subscribed to the oath required. It was a hard thing but the only alternative. Women and children are also required to swear allegiance or be prisoners at home.

I am now a prisoner at home, liable to be arrested if I but leave the yard. God being my help, I will not take the oath unless circumstances beyond my control force me to it".

Sexual Violence

Fear of rape surely chilled the hearts of white women in the South, during the War. The scant documentation available indicates however, that African American women, usually slaves or freed slaves, suffered most.

One diarist a former slave, Harriet Jacobs, lived 29 years as a slave, seven of which were spent in a cramped hiding place to escape a sexually predatory master.

Facts are hard to come by. In the Victorian 1860s, sexual crimes against women were kept behind a curtain of silence to protect reputations of the delicate sex.

The Union army did keep records. President Lincoln's order known as the *Lieber Code of 1863*, set clear rules for engaging with enemy combatants. This code declared that occupying soldiers would "acknowledge and protect, in hostile countries... that "all rape, wounding, maiming, or killing of such inhabitants, are prohibited under the penalty of death."

Most attacks occurred during Sherman's March to the Sea.

Union military courts prosecuted at least 450 cases involving sexual crimes:

In North Carolina during the spring of 1865, Pvt. James Preble "did by physical force and violence commit rape upon the person of one Miss Letitia Craft." He as court-martialed.

When Perry Holland of the 1st Missouri Infantry confessed to the rape of Julia Anderson, a white woman in Tennessee, he was sentenced to be shot, but his sentence was later commuted.

Catherine Farmer, also of Tennessee, testified that Lt. Harvey John of the 49th Ohio Infantry dragged her into the bushes and told her he would kill her if she did not "give it to him." He tore her dress, broke her hoops and "put his private parts into her," for which he was sentenced to 10 years in prison

North Carolina:
A Union soldier was tried and hanged for the rape of a 58-year-old woman in Wayne County. Reports indicate army "stragglers ravished" women between Kinston and Goldsboro.

While black women may have been particularly vulnerable to wartime rape, the Lieber Code brought them for the first time under the umbrella of legal protection. So black women were more protected legally from rape during war time, then previously as slaves. Some black women were able to mobilize military law to their advantage.

In the summer of 1864, Jenny Green, a young "colored" girl who had escaped slavery and sought refuge with the Union Army in Richmond, Va., was brutally raped by Lt. Andrew J. Smith, 11th Pennsylvania Cavalry.

She brought charges against him, and she testified in a military court. "He threw me on the floor, pulled up my dress," she told the all- male tribunal He did what married people do. I am but a child."

The idea that a former slave, and an adolescent girl at that, could demand and receive legal redress was revolutionary. Smith was discharged from the Army and sentenced to 10 years of hard labor.

Georgia: Near Milledgeville, two Union soldiers raped Kate Nichols, wife of a Confederate captain. Nichols went insane and spent the rest of her life in an asylum. The rapists, possibly a pair among the horde of ravaging "bummers" following Sherman's troops, were not captured.

New Orleans: When the Union took New Orleans in 1862, Major Gen. Benjamin Butler ordered his men to treat the taunting Southern white women as if they were prostitutes. We might guess the results of Butler's order.

In the spring of 1863, John N. Williams of the 7th Tennessee Regiment wrote in his diary, "Heard from home. The Yankees has been through there. Seem to be their object to commit rape on every Negro woman they can find."

Evacuation

Phoebe Pember
A Southern Woman's Story
The following is an account of the evacuation of Fredericksburg, Virginia.

"The quarter-master's and commissary's stores were thrown open and thousands of the half- starved and half-clad people of Richmond rushed to the scene.

Delicate women tottered under the weight of hams, bags of coffee, flour and sugar. Invalided officers carried away articles of unaccustomed luxury for sick wives and children at home.

Government employees, speculators, gamblers, strangers, pleasure and profit lovers of all kinds ...were "packing...

The scene at the station was of indescribable confusion. No one could afford to abandon any article of wear or household use, when going where they knew that nothing could be replaced. Baggage was as valuable as life".

Sarah Morgan
Dawson Louisiana
A Confederate Girl's Diary
Sarah was born to a wealthy, influential family. Sarah, her mother, and her sisters moved back and forth between Baton Rouge and the surrounding countryside during the early war years. In 1862 the threat of further violence forced them to abandon their home in Baton Rouge an temporarily seek shelter with friends. Lack of food and their mother's ill health later forced them to relocate to an occupied New Orleans.

"I found Lilly (a family friend) wild with excitement, picking up hastily whatever came to hand, preparing for instant flight, she knew not where. The Yankees were in sight; the town was to be burned; we were to run to the woods, etc. If the house had to be burned, I had to make up my mind to run, too. So my treasure-bag tied around my waist as a bustle, a sack with a few necessary articles hanging on my arm, some few quite unnecessary ones, too.

... I suppose I am as wild as the rest. It is nonsense to tell me I am cool, with all these patriotic and enthusiastic sentiments. Nothing can be positively ascertained, save that our gunboats are sunk, and theirs are coming up to the city...we really do not know whether the city has been taken or not. We only know we had best be prepared for anything. So day before yesterday, Lilly and I sewed up our jewelry, which may be of use if we have to fly.

...This is a dreadful war, to make even the hearts of women so bitter! I hardly know myself these last few weeks. I, who have such a horror of bloodshed, consider even killing in self-defense murder, who cannot wish them the slightest evil, whose only prayer is to have them sent back in peace to their own country... I talk of killing them!

For what else do I wear a pistol and carving-knife? I am afraid I will try them on the first one who says an insolent word to me. Yes, and repent for it ever after in sack-cloth and ashes...if I was only a man!...these are evidently gentlemen...

Although a strong supporter of the Confederacy, when Yankees captured New Orleans in 1862, Morgan was at first impressed with civility of the Union officers. Sarah does not hesitate to record the kindness of some members of the Union Army. Her feelings were complex, she retained bitter feelings too. She concludes that rudeness and are not becoming of a southern lady:

"Fine, noble-looking men they were, showing refinement and gentlemanly bearing in every motion. One cannot help but admire such foes!"

Sarah Lois Wadley
Diary, August 8, 1859 - May 15, 1865:
Sarah's father was the superintendent of
railroads for the Confederacy. Her family
spent the war in Louisiana and Georgia. Her
diary shows how Southern women helped
each other, even if their own resources were
few.

"Mrs. Stone (a lady from the swamp) came to
Mother to get board for herself and family for
a week; they had escaped from the swamp in
haste and at night, lost all their clothing,
except what was contained in one small
trunk, and abandoned their house and
furniture entirely to the Yankees and negroes.

Mother was very reluctant to take them, but
they urged it and she could not refuse
persons in their situation, so they came".

Eliza Ripley
*From Flag to Flag, A Woman's Adventures
and Experiences in the South during the War,
in Mexico, and in Cuba*

Fleeing from Louisiana to Texas
Eliza spent an idyllic childhood among
the privileged upper class in New
Orleans, Louisiana. She narrowly
escaped the approach of the Union
Army in 1862 by quickly evacuating to
Texas with her husband and their two
children, Henry and an infant son. They
eventually emigrate to Cuba, where they
run a sugar plantation.

Pickets at every corner
A Picket is a soldier, or small unit of soldiers,
placed in front of the army. They kept a

'vigilant watch' over the front lines, and over the movements of the enemy.

"By evening we reached the end of Gartness Lane, and a black head popped out of the bushes. *'Don't go dat road, pickets down dar!'* so we turned up the road we wanted to go down."

A few decrepit, bedraggled, dejected women, with whole families of shivering children, walked the dusty roadside.

These were the "rear-guard," as it were, of a little army of wretched citizens fleeing from their broken homes. ... We were going to Texas,
the great State that opened its hospitable doors to hundreds of refugees fleeing like ourselves".

The northern troops seemed to act with malice:
"The grand portraits, heirlooms of that aristocratic family, men of the Revolutionary period, high-bred dames of a long-past generation in short bodices, puffed sleeves, ... - these portraits hung upon the walls, slashed by swords clear across from side to side, stabbed and mutilated in every brutal way!

The contents of store-closets had been poured over the floors; molasses and vinegar, and everything that defaces and stains, had been smeared over walls and furniture. Up-stairs,

armoires with mirror-doors had been
smashed in with heavy axes or hammers, and
the dainty dresses of the young ladies torn
and crushed with studied, painstaking
malignity".

Poignant leave-taking:
"I wandered through the dear old rooms of
the house where we had lived ten happy years,
taking a mournful farewell of a
whole *armoire* of dinner and ball dresses, that
were of no use to me now".

Emancipation

Emancipated slaves

During the Civil War, hundreds of slaves were released from bondage by Union forces before they were officially freed by the Emancipation Proclamation. There was no clear federal policy at that time concerning freed slaves; individual commanders made their own decisions as to how to handle this peculiar form of "contraband."

Freedom was a new state of being and justifiably some former slaves moved hesitantly into this new world. Others ran toward it with open arms.

For many plantation owners, the prospect of freed men and women was confusing and frightening. Some reacted with rage, others with compassion and concern. Others had ambiguous feelings.

"...the emancipation of the slaves. How is that going to be dealt with? We who know them, and have learned to love them and care for them since we were children, cannot foresee what their freedom will bring to them. While I rejoice that they have it, I pity them, for they are in no way prepared for it... I am sure that they will all want to go back to the plantation, for they hate Texas and long to return to the sugar-cane and warmth of Louisiana. James has written to the overseer to give them the necessary money to take them back if they wish to go.". *Francis Hewitt Fearn*

Freed slaves had to figure out what it would mean to live in the United States as citizens rather than property.

Former slave, W.L. Bost:
"Then after the war was over we was afraid
to move. Jes like tarpins or turtles after
'mancipation. Jes stick our heads out to see
how the land lay. My mammy stay with
Marse Jonah for 'bout a year after freedom
then ole Solomon Hall made her an offer".

Some historians have reservations about the
reliability of the "Slave Narratives" recorded
during the 1930s. More than seventy years
elapsed between Emancipation and the
interviews. Most informants had experienced
slavery only as children or adolescents. In the
tough Depression years of the 1930s, when
the interviews took place, the past might be

colored with nostalgia. These factors often combined to make them look upon the past through rose- colored glasses.

Yet these eyewitness accounts of former slaves are valuable sources, they offer a glimpse into another time and world.

Clara C. Young
Former slave
Mississippi Federal Writers Project
Clara was not fond of the Yankees. She stayed on the plantation after freedom came.

"De Yankees come 'roun' afte' de War an' tol' us we's fre (free) an' we shouted an' sang, an' had a big celebration fer a few days.

Den we got to wonderin' 'bout what good it did us. It didn' feel no diffrunt.

We all loved our marster an' missus an' stayed on wid 'em jes' lak nothin' had happened. We didn' lak de Yankees anyway. Dey wa'nt (weren't) good to us; when dey lef' we would allus sing dat leetle song what go lak dis:

'Old Mister Yankee, think he is so grand,
Wid his blue coat tail
a draggin' on de ground!'

I stayed on wid Old Marster afte' de surrender".

Jane Sutton
Former Slave, Gulfport, Mississippi. *Federal Writer's Project*
Jane Sutton also found it difficult to leave her Master, for whom she expresses fondness. The plantation was the only life she had known.

"When the Yankees came she hid all the hams and meats.

Dey didn' git much. Dey was so mad dey jus' tore up some of Old Mis' clo'es (clothes) what was in de wardrobe. Us was sho' scairt of 'em.

"I 'members dey promise to give de cullud folks all kin' o' things. Dey never give 'em nothin' dat I know's about. Us was jus' turnt loose to scratch for us ownse'ves.

Us was glad to stay on wid de white folks, 'cause dey was de bes' frien's us had. I don' know nobody what got a thing 'cept what Old Marster an' Old Mis' give 'em.

He (the Master) used to bring us candy whan he went to town. Us'd be lookin' for 'im when he come home. He'd say, 'Whars all my little Niggers?' Den us'd come a-runnin' an' he'd han' it to us out-a his saddle bags. It was mos'ly good stick candy."

Hannah Austin
Federal Writers Project
Hannah welcomed freedom. In this account, she describes her distaste for the Yankees as they steal her master's property. However, later when her Mistress makes demands on her, she adamantly tells her Mistress that she was now free and is no longer obligated.

"Yankee Army appeared in our village one day They practically destroyed Mr Hall's store by throwing all clothes and other merchandise into the streets.

Seeing my sister and I they turned to us saying 'Little Negroes you are free there are no more masters and mistresses. Here help yourselves to these clothes take them home with you'.

Not knowing any better, we carried stockings, socks, dresses, underwear and many other pieces home. After this they opened the smoke house door and told us to go in and take all of the meat we wanted.

On another occasion the mistress called me asking that I come in the yard to play with the children.

I did not go but politely told her I was free and didn't belong to anyone but my mama and papa. As I spoke these words my mistress began to cry".

Civil War Recipes

Lacking many ingredients, the southern women learned to alter food recipes according to their scarce available resources.

The only Southern cookbook of the war years was *The Confederate Receipt Book*.
Published in 1863, it had a revealing subtitle:
"A Compilation of over one hundred receipts adapted to the times."

And those were the worst of times, most miserably manifested in a recipe for Apple Pie without apples: "To one small bowl of crackers that have been soaked until no hard parts remain, add one teaspoonful of tartaric acid, sweeten to your taste, add some butter, and a very little nutmeg."

What remained plentiful in the South were protein-rich peanuts and black-eyed peas, both of which, ironically enough, were brought from West Africa by the very slaves over whom the war was being fought.

Old Fashioned Oatmeal Pie
The following recipe provides flavors that substitute for pecans, which were hard to find. A very frugal recipe and tasty.

Ingredients:
1 (9 inch) pie crust
4 eggs
1 cup sugar
2 tablespoons flour
1 teaspoon ground cinnamon
1/4 teaspoon salt
1 cup light corn syrup
1/8 to 1/4 cup melted
butter 1 teaspoon vanilla

1 cup quick cooking oatmeal (uncooked)

Directions:
Preheat oven 350 degrees. Beat eggs until frothy. Combine sugar, flour, cinnamon, and salt in small bowl. Add eggs and mix well. Add corn syrup, melted butter and vanilla. Mix oatmeal. Pour into uncooked pie shell. Bake for 45 minutes.

Cabbage Stew
Ingredients:
1 head green cabbage
Onions
Salt pork (cut into cubes)
Stewed tomatoes
Salt, garlic salt, pepper, Cajun seasoning or ground red pepper

Instructions

Fry the salt pork in a large pot until well
browned (do not drain). Turn the heat down
Add cabbage and cook until wilted
Add onions and cook until wilted

Let cook approximately 1 hour (low fire).
Add tomatoes.   Simmer.

Add a little garlic salt, then add salt and
pepper to taste. Add small amount of Cajun
seasoning or ground red pepper. Stir
occasionally. After approximately 2-3 hours,
taste, and season and/or cook more if
necessary.

Molasses Cookies
Ingredients:
1/3 cup brown sugar
1/3 cup shortening
1 egg
2/3 cup molasses

2 ¾ cup
flour 2 tsp
cinnamon
1 tsp ginger
1 tsp baking
soda 1 tsp salt

Instructions:
Cream together shortening, brown sugar, egg, and molasses. Stir in flour, baking soda, salt, cinnamon, and ginger. Chill in the refrigerator for at least one hour.

Heat the oven to 375 degrees and roll dough out to 1/4". Cut out cookies with a round cookie cutter (can use edge of a glass, or a lid). Place on a baking sheet; bake for 10 minutes.

The Soldier's Food

The daily rations were given to the soldiers uncooked. Generals and other officers had the luxury of a cook, but the vast majority of soldiers gathered in small groups each evening to prepare their food. The food was low quality for both armies, but the Confederate soldier suffered more from lack of food.

Civil War soldiers did occasionally obtain fresh meat by foraging or plunder. When in enemy territory, they took cattle, pigs, sheep and chickens, and frequently helped themselves to fruit, vegetables, and other items from local farms. Commanders might reprimand soldiers for such acts, but this seldom stopped a hungry man from seeking extra food.

The North – Union Army

Hardtack

Hardtack was generally eaten by the northern army. The soldier's typical diet: salt pork, hardtack, occasional dried vegetables and coffee.

Hard as a rock, this cracker was the bane of many a Civil War soldier. Soldiers called the hard little biscuits, "tooth-dullers", and "worm castles" because there were often weevils and maggots in the crackers.

Hardtack was almost inedible and nearly dense enough to stop a musket ball. To soften, it was often dunked in brine, coffee, or cooked with salt pork.

Recipe
Ingredients:

2 cups of flour
1/2 to 3/4 cup water
6 pinches of salt

Optional: add 1 tbsp of vegetable fat

Preheat oven to 400 degrees F.

Mix the ingredients together into a stiff dough, knead several times, and spread the dough out flat to a thickness of 1/4 inch on a non-greased cookie sheet.

Using a knife, cut dough into 3-inch cracker squares. Punch four rows of holes, four holes per row, into each cracker.

Bake for 30 minutes. Remove from oven, turn crackers over on the sheet and return to the oven and bake another 30 minutes. Cool completely.

The South - Confederate Army

For the most part, rations consisted of bad beef and cornbread. Confederate soldiers usually didn't receive much food at all especially as the war dragged on.

At times there was no meat, and rice and molasses was recommended as a substitute. Beginning in 1863, mule meat was issued to soldiers. There are many reports of men existing on handfuls of parched corn and field peas for days.

Confederate Cush or Coosh
Cush was a thick mush, similar in consistency to oatmeal porridge, that was made by cooking bacon in a frying pan, then adding water and cornmeal.

Ingredients
Fat bacon
Cubed cooked beef
Cornmeal mush
1 qt water
1 clove garlic (optional)

Directions:

Chop up a small quantity of fat bacon. Put into a hot iron skillet and fry. (Remove extra grease). Add beef. Slowly add a quart of water. When it boils, add cornmeal mush and stir until dry. Remove skillet from fire. Wait until it cools. Serve warm, like hash. (If more water is added, it can serve as a stew.)

Johnny Cakes
Confederate soldiers had more access to corn than flour and ate more Johnny Cakes than Hardtack.

Recipe
1 cup cornmeal
½ teaspoon salt
1 ¼ cup boiling water
Tablespoon bacon
drippings or vegetable oil

(Optional: add ½ cup milk and/or 2 tablespoons molasses)

Directions
1. Mix the cornmeal, and salt together.
2. Slowly add the boiling water to the cornmeal.
3. Dribble batter on the griddle to make cakes.
4. After the edges dry, wait about 30 seconds and then flip the Johnny-cake over with a wide spatula.

Serve warm with butter, maple syrup, molasses, gravy, or baked beans, if available.

Johnny Cakes can also be baked in the oven. Bake on a lightly greased sheet at 350°F for 20 - 25 minutes or until golden brown

Sloosh

Many soldiers simply cooked cornmeal mush around a rifle ramrod. "Sloosh" was a mixture of cornmeal, lard or bacon, water and egg formed around a rifle ramrod and cooked over a campfire.

Christmas and Holiday food

Food was scarce for the South, but they tried to celebrate Christmas and the Holidays. Here is a frugal recipe used for party cakes in the South.

Idiot's Delight Cake

This cake was popular because it used only a few, inexpensive, easy to obtain ingredients. It was called *Idiots Delight* because it was so easy to make. This deep-dish, biscuit-like dessert floating in a thick cinnamon-raisin sauce.

Ingredients:

Filling:
1 c. brown
sugar 1 c.
raisins
1 tbsp. butter
1 tsp. vanilla
4 c. water

Batter:
7 tbsp. butter
1/2 c. white
sugar
2 tsp. baking
powder 1/2 c. milk
1 c. flour

Boil together the first 5 ingredients. Make a batter of the butter, sugar, baking powder, milk and flour. Drop the batter in a greased pan by spoonful. Pour first mixture over it and bake in a moderate oven until golden brown.
Source: <u>Cooks.com</u>

Hoppin' John

"Hoppin John" is a traditional southern New Year's Day dish made of black-eyed peas.

Ingredients

1 1/2 cups dried black-eyed peas 8 cups water, divided
3 teaspoons
salt 1 small
ham hock
5 slices of thick cut
bacon 1 large onion, chopped
2 cups long-grain white rice,

uncooked 1 teaspoon dried red
pepper flakes

Directions
Over medium heat, place the dried black-
eyed peas, 6 cups of water, salt and ham hock.
Cook covered over medium heat until tender,
about 2-2 1/2 hours.

While the peas are cooking, fry the bacon until
crisp. Remove bacon, crumble and set aside,
reserving the bacon grease.

Sauté chopped onion in the bacon grease until softened. In a large sized sauce pan, add the rice, 2 cups of the pea liquid, 2 cups of water, 2 cups of the cooked black-eyed peas, sautéed onions, bacon grease, crumbled bacon and red pepper flakes.

Cook covered over medium-low heat until rice is done, about 15-20 minutes.
Source: SheWearsManyHats.com

Artificial oysters
In truth, these don't taste exactly like oysters, they are more like small corn fritters, but the texture is very similar to oysters.

Recipe

2 cups of young corn (*cooked, grated from cob &
  mashed*)
3 tbsp flour
2 eggs, beaten
1 tsp salt
Pinch of black pepper
Pinch of cayenne pepper
Butter or oil for frying

Mix together first 5 ingredients. Fry in
shallow oil or butter until golden brown on
each side.

A tablespoonful of the batter will make the
size of an oyster. Fry them until light brown,
and when done butter them. Cream, if it can
be procured, is even better.

Conclusion

The experiences during the war would affect the generations to come.

"For women, the Civil War provided an opportunity for some to step out of nineteenth century gender roles, although the war did not provoke any major redefinition of women's sphere. Women were still unable to hold office or vote and were thus outside the political process in those capacities.

Yet during the Civil War, they participated politically by attending rallies, joining Ladies' Aid Societies, circulating petitions, and organizing fund-raising campaigns.

They ran farms and businesses. They were witnesses, writers, soldiers, smugglers, nurses, cooks, laundresses, prostitutes, and mourners". *Crossroads of War,* http://crossroadsofwar.org

For the slave woman, a new life of possibilities lay at the horizon. Freed from the atrocities of slavery, no longer to lose her children, no longer violated, her life would never be the same.

A popular southern painting of the era hints at this social transformation. The painting is a portrayal of loyalty and sacrifice to the Confederate cause, but it subtly reveals the altering roles of women.

The painting is entitled *The Burial of Latane.* It was painted in 1864 by William D. Washington (a descendant of George Washington).

In the painting, white women, slaves, and children perform the burial service of a Confederate cavalry officer Lt William Latane. The fallen hero died among strangers, surrounded by enemy forces, unable to summon his family or a minister to perform the service. The women have come to entomb the victim of the "supreme sacrifice".

It is a significant painting: the principal figures are only slaves and women. The only white male is dead. A woman serves as Preacher, and is placed in a role of power, previously given to men. Women are now political actors in their society. The painting makes specific statements about gender and race and new roles. Social relations were truly in a state of transformation.

Some women never recovered from the wartime taste of autonomy. Before the war, their lives were about conforming to the strict Southern code of womanhood. White elite men had power over women, lower class whites, and slaves. However, a new distrust of the men who could no longer protect them, drove Confederate women towards a new independence, whether they wanted to embrace it or not.

~~~~~~~~~~~~~~~~~~

The Confederacy had lost around 260,000 men. 93,000 were killed in combat, disease killed the rest. The War created an unprecedented number of young widows, many of whom had been married for a very short time. Many had hurried to marry their loved ones before they marched off to war.

Beginning in 1888, some widows were eligible for a state pension of $30 per year.

Once it was verified that the soldier husband was dead, the long ordeal of mourning began. Black silk dresses and heavy veils were expensive and sometimes hard to find.

During the Civil War so many women wore black that it often seemed that the entire nation was cloaked in dark shadows. The ideal Civil War widow wore all black clothing and mourned for a minimum of two and a half years.

Then there was the "flirty widow", and flirting could lead to an early remarriage. Of course, most of American society did not believe that young widows must remain single forever.

Most sanctioned remarriage after the respectable amount of time - thirty months - had passed, but some young widows were unable or unwilling to wait that long.

Observing a flirty widow on a train, a stranger remarked to diarist Mary Boykin Chesnut: "As soon as she began whining about her dead beau I knew she was after another one..."

On a more serious note, when the battlefields fell silent, the women's work had only begun. They were left to heal and nurture shattered husbands, sons, and fathers, and they needed all their strength to raise the next generation, both at home and in the schoolroom.

Something rises above the misery of war, the aching poverty, the unbearable sorrow, the humiliation. Women found this inner stream and it sustained and ran through their lives and bestowed beautiful legacies to their families.

Americans must see their lives with a great sense of honor and wonder.

~~~~~~~~~~~~~~~~~~~

A Love Letter from the Front

And now, from the misery and horror of war, we end with love. "The following is a love letter from soldier Sullivan Ballao to his wife Sarah, as he waits to enter the first battle of Bull Run:

July the 14th, 1861   Washington DC

My very dear Sarah:

The indications are very strong that we shall move in a few days..., I feel impelled to write lines that may fall under your eye when I shall be no more.

... If it is necessary that I should fall on the battlefield for my country, I am ready.

I, suspicious that Death is creeping behind me with his fatal dart, am communing with God, my country, and thee.
....
Sarah, my love for you is deathless.
....
But, O Sarah! If the dead can come back to this earth and flit unseen around those they loved, I shall always be near you; in the garish day and in the darkest night -- amidst your happiest scenes and gloomiest hours ...

Sarah, do not mourn me dead; think I am gone and wait for thee, for we shall meet again.

As for my little boys, they will grow as I have done, and never know a father's love and care. ... Sarah, I have unlimited confidence in your maternal care and your development of their characters.

Tell my two mothers his and hers I call God's blessing upon them. O Sarah, I wait for you there!

Come to me, and lead thither my children.

~Sullivan

Sullivan Ballao died at the battle of Bull Run on July 21, 1861. When he died, his wife was 24.

~~~~~~~~~~~~~

On April 9, 1865, the Civil War officially came to an end in Appomattox, Va., when Confederate General Robert E. Lee surrendered to Union General Ulysses S. Grant.

~end~

If you enjoyed this book, would you be kind enough to leave a review for this book on Amazon? Greatly appreciated!

contact author:
email: safeinthewoods@gmail.com

visit our website:
http://hearth-hardship.blogspot.com/